Keeping It Light

ISMS That Inspire, Motivate, Build Culture
and Make Tough Decisions a Breeze

David Paddison

&

Larry G. Linne

Contents

Acknowledgements from David

I want to thank some special people who helped make this book a reality. First of all, to my wife Jeanne, she is the long-suffering victim who hears these sayings over and over – I fear that if there is a repetitive injury condition related to eye rolling, she will get it. To my children, who also have suffered, I am grateful for your putting up with them as well. It is a heart-warming feeling for me when I hear them repeating some of my advice to their friends! As they have grown, I have earned a parenting promotion from "Fun Sucker" during their adolescence to "Dream Crusher" in their adult life and I am thankful for that too.

I couldn't do any of this without the loyal support of the team at Sterling Seacrest Pritchard. They have to put up with me more than they deserve and do so with the understanding that it may take a minute to connect the dots to the current situation, but if they take a breath and avoid the urge to strike, there may be a small morsel in there that can help us navigate a tricky situation to the betterment of all concerned. 19 years, no fights, but more than a few "what did he just say?" moments that could have gone poorly.

The group that really threw the party for this effort is my clients and insurance carrier partners. We have all had our share of tense moments that have been eased by applying these principles and working collaboratively to find solutions. 40 plus years, plenty of fights, but nothing more than a flesh wound on occasion. The ability to develop these sayings and apply them in the real world is all their doing. Learning, growing, and navigating the tough things in life together has provided the crucible to test my thoughts in real-world dynamic environments.

Just to be transparent, this book contains the ones that worked – the cutting room floor is littered with close calls and approaches that fell flat when put to the test. Learn and move on, but never forget the situation and the solution; it will come back around in a similar form down the road.

A special shout-out to Larry Linne – he made the tragic mistake of helping me get all of this on paper and is probably sorry he did. Being a get'er done guy, he soldiered through the phone calls, video conferences, emails, and text messages to try to comprehend the unorganized mess that is my stream of consciousness. I am so glad he did.

Most of my isms are cobbled together from a lot of different sources and experiences, and Larry was uniquely able to sift through all of it and extract the essence of the ones that he believed would help other people the most on their life journey. I didn't expect that our efforts would ever result in anything I would read or possibly share, but I am so happy that Larry cracked the code and hope you enjoy the fruits of his labors because without him, none of this would have made it onto paper.

About the Authors

David Paddison is the President of Sterling Seacrest Pritchard and has been a respected leader in the insurance agency industry for more than 30 years. Known for his passion for developing people, David helps others become the best versions of themselves. He is recognized for his unique ability to distill life and leadership lessons into memorable "ISMS" — practical tools that make success principles simple to understand and easy to apply. His approach has inspired countless individuals across his companies and in his community.

A native of Savannah, Georgia, David was recently inducted into the Savannah Business Hall of Fame. His commitment to service extends beyond business, as he has devoted his time to numerous non-profit boards and to mentoring the next generation of leaders.

Larry G. Linne is the CEO at InCite Performance Group and is known internationally as a thought leader in business strategy and executive development. After a career in the NFL, Larry has led businesses and authored many top-selling books like "Make the Noise Go Away – The Power of An Effective Second in Command", "Brand Aid – Taking Control of Your Reputation Before Everyone Else Does", and "Leading Performance Because It Can't Be Managed – How to Lead the Modern Workforce". He has been the co-author for rEvolution by Tim Leman, Resigned to Success by Scott White, and contributed to numerous other business and life success books. Larry is a highly regarded speaker due to his business acumen and sports experiences.

Larry lives in northern Colorado with his wife, Deborah. They have 5 daughters and currently have 5 grandchildren.

Preface

I met David Paddison in a hotel restaurant and bar in 2016. I was in Atlanta the night before teaching a sales training class for his firm. He was the President of Sterling Seacrest Partners. He had been the CEO of Seacrest Partners in Savannah, Georgia. After a merger with Sterling Risk Advisors from Atlanta, he assumed the President role of the new, large regional insurance agency. Through continued acquisition, the company name is now Sterling Seacrest Pritchard, and they have become a leading national insurance agency.

Prior to meeting David, I was informed that he had more "isms" than anyone I would ever meet. They informed me that the "isms" were known as Paddisonisms! I had never heard of the term "isms" and wasn't sure what I was going to face. I googled "isms" and learned that isms represent systems, philosophies and practices. I still had no idea what to expect, but I can say that evening at the bar was one of the most enjoyable discussions I have had in my career.

David had a story for every point that was made in the discussion. He could refer to quips, stories, old sayings and had the timing and charm of a brilliant stand-up comic.

However, these weren't just cute, memorable sayings to David. These were principles he lived by, taught and expected in his life and of others. These principles had become the foundation of who he is as a leader. It was like he had built clear icons for everything he believed in so he could remember and maintain that belief.

I went to my hotel room after three hours of discussions and wrote down everything I could remember. I later learned it was only a fraction of the isms David had in his head.

In 2022, I had the opportunity to invite David to be a presenter on a panel for leadership and perpetuation. I interviewed David in preparation and learned I could have had him as the only person on stage. David was brilliant and the entire audience was buzzing about his ideas and entertaining quips.

When we walked off stage, I turned to David and asked if he ever thought of sharing all of his great isms in a book. He smiled big and said, "I have always wanted to put all of these ideas in a book, but I am not a writer." I told him it would be an honor to help him put the isms in a book for leaders to read and use in their future businesses.

We started our journey a few months later and I found it fascinating. He would share his isms, and I would add quips, stories, similar ideas, and my experiences to enhance and round out the thoughts.

We continued this for a few months, and we found the joint work could be valuable to readers. He agreed that I should add my stories and additions to his isms as well as my own isms. He was gracious and said he didn't even care if his name was on the book. I will assure you, 75% of this book is David Paddison's brilliance. My contributions are only there to enhance clarity, throw in some of my experiences and to create proof of concept to his library of inspiration.

I hope you enjoy our collective inspirational isms and hopefully gain great value from the wild brain of David Paddison.

Chapter 1
Enough is Enough

Success is not about knowing everything, being the absolute best, or preparing indefinitely. It's about knowing when you have *enough*, enough knowledge, enough skill, enough preparation, to move forward. The pursuit of perfection can become the very thing that holds us back.

There's a balance between being prepared and being *overprepared*. When you cross the line into overpreparation, you slow yourself down. You get stuck in analysis paralysis, seeking more data, more insight, more certainty, when in reality, you already have *enough* to take action.

The Power of Enough

Know Enough – You don't have to be the smartest person in the room. The best leaders and decision makers don't have all the answers, but they know how to find them when needed.

Good Enough – Perfection is the enemy of progress. If you wait until something is flawless, you'll never launch, never move, and never succeed.

Smart Enough – Intelligence is valuable, but knowing how to apply what you know is far more important than simply accumulating knowledge.

Close Enough – In most cases, being 90% ready is more than sufficient. You can adapt and refine as you go.

Fast Enough – Speed matters. Being prepared is important, but overpreparation can make you slow to seize opportunities.

High Enough – Sometimes, reaching a little further isn't worth the delay. Success comes from knowing when to stop climbing and start executing.

Knowing Enough to Lead Experts

A strong leader doesn't need to be the most knowledgeable person in the room, but she does need to *know enough* to effectively guide those who are. Without sufficient knowledge, she won't know what questions to ask, what assumptions to challenge, or how to navigate critical decisions.

As a CEO leading a team of data scientists, she doesn't need to be an expert in coding, machine learning, or statistical modeling, but she does need to understand enough about the field to:

Ask the right questions that drive innovation and problem-solving.

Identify potential roadblocks before they become crises.

Challenge assumptions to push the team toward better solutions.

Bridge the gap between technical expertise and business strategy.

By having *enough* knowledge, she becomes a leadership catalyst, someone who can extract the best insights from her team, push for clarity and creativity, and ultimately drive a great outcome. The leader who knows *nothing* is ineffective. The leader who tries to know *everything* slows progress. The leader who knows *enough* unlocks the full potential of her team.

The Trap of Knowing Too Much

Trying to be a *know-it-all* isn't just exhausting, it's counterproductive. It makes you too specialized, too rigid, and often too disconnected from those around you. People don't respect arrogance, and they certainly don't appreciate someone who always needs to prove they are the smartest person in the room.

The most successful people understand that knowing *enough* is what allows them to move forward with confidence. Give yourself 15 minutes, and you can go from *enough* to the *answer*. You don't need a lifetime of preparation to make a great decision; you just need to be ready *enough* to take the next step.

Embracing the Mindset of Enough

Knowing when you have enough is an art. It requires confidence, adaptability and trust in yourself.

Overpreparation leads to hesitation, while knowing when to move leads to progress.

The question is: Are you holding yourself back by waiting for more when you already have *enough* to succeed?

Chapter 2
Harm's Way is The Only Way

In the world of leadership, success often appears to be a matter of strategy, skill, or timing. But beneath these surface-level factors lies a deeper truth: the greatest value we have as human beings resides within the risks we are willing to take.

Leadership is not about avoiding discomfort or guaranteeing outcomes; it is about stepping into uncertainty with conviction, even when the path ahead is unclear.

Richard, a mid-level manager at a tech startup, had ideas about how to streamline his team's workflow for years, but he hesitated to speak up.

"What if my ideas don't work?" he thought. *"What if I look foolish in front of my peers or superiors?"* These fears kept him playing it safe, sticking to the status quo.

But one day, faced with a looming project deadline and a growing sense of frustration, Richard decided to take a risk. He called an impromptu meeting and laid out his plan to overhaul the team's processes.

The response was mixed; some colleagues were skeptical, others intrigued. Yet, by taking that initial risk, Richard set in motion a transformation. Over time, his ideas gained traction, and the team's productivity soared. His willingness to step out of his comfort zone didn't just solve a problem, it redefined him as a leader.

Why Risk Matters

Risk is the currency of growth. When we take risks, we signal to ourselves and others that we value progress over perfection. Risks challenge our assumptions, force us to innovate, and push us to discover what we're truly capable of. Without risk, there is no movement, only stagnation.

Consider the greatest leaders in history. From Rosa Parks to Jeff Bezos, their value wasn't in their ability to follow the safest path; their value was in their courage to take the leap, even when failure seemed more likely than success. Rosa Parks risked her life to fight for civil rights. Jeff Bezos quit his job and started a bookstore out of his garage that could have easily failed. These leaders were defined not by guarantees but by their willingness to embrace uncertainty.

The Fear Barrier

Risk is uncomfortable. It's natural to fear failure, rejection or criticism, but the greatest barriers to success aren't external; they're internal. The stories we tell ourselves about why we can't take a risk are often the only things standing in our way.

To overcome the fear barrier, leaders must reframe their relationship with fear. Fear is not a stop sign; it's a guidepost pointing us toward opportunities for growth. When we feel fear, it's often a sign that we're on the brink of something important. The key is to act in spite of it.

The Legacy of Risk

The risks we take define not only our leadership but also our legacy. When we look back on our lives, we won't remember the moments we played it safe. We'll remember the leaps we took, the challenges we embraced and endured, and the growth we achieved as a result. Our value as leaders, and as human beings, resides not in what we avoid but in what we're willing to risk.

Chapter 3
Beware of Predicting the
Consequences of the Future

Life's challenges are inevitable. From heartbreak to financial struggles, moments of crisis seem to descend like storms, unbidden and uncontrollable. Yet, what if the pain we feel isn't from the events themselves but from the stories we craft about what those events mean for our future?

Sitting in her apartment, Maya stared at the eviction notice taped to her front door. The bright red letters screamed **"FINAL NOTICE,"** underscoring the magnitude of her failure. Her chest tightened, her breath became shallow. She wasn't just losing her home, she thought, she was losing everything: her dignity, her security, and her future.

"What now?" she whispered to herself.

As despair took hold, Maya's mind painted vivid pictures of her future. She saw herself homeless, cold, and hungry. She imagined the pitying glances of former coworkers and the judgment of friends who would surely think she hadn't worked hard enough. **"How did I let this happen?"** she asked herself over and over again.

But then, a memory surfaced, a conversation with her grandmother.

"Maya," her grandmother had said, *"Pain doesn't come from what happens to us. It comes from what we tell ourselves about it. The future you fear doesn't exist yet, but your thoughts make it feel real."*

Maya took a deep breath and decided to challenge the story she was telling herself. She grabbed a notebook and wrote down her fears:

1. I will end up homeless.

2. Everyone will think I'm a failure.

3. I'll never recover from this.

Once her fears were on paper, they looked less insurmountable. She began to question each one:

- **Will I really end up homeless?** I have friends who would let me stay with them. I have options I haven't explored yet.

- **Will everyone think I'm a failure?** People have their own lives and struggles; they're not spending their time judging mine.

- **Will I never recover?** This isn't the first hard thing I've faced. I've overcome challenges before, and I'll do it again.

By confronting her thoughts, Maya began to feel a shift. The situation hadn't changed; the eviction notice was still there, but her suffering started to lift. She realized she wasn't defeated; she was at a crossroads. And while she couldn't control the storm, she could choose how to navigate through it.

The Power of Perspective

The human mind is an extraordinary storyteller. It takes raw facts, a breakup, a job loss, a diagnosis, and weaves intricate narratives about what those facts mean. These stories shape our emotions and dictate our actions. Yet, too often, we forget that we are the authors of these stories, not mere characters at their mercy.

When we face hardship, our default response is often to catastrophize. A failed relationship becomes *"I'll never find love again."* A missed promotion turns into *"I'm destined to fail in my career."* These stories aren't truths; they're interpretations, and interpretations can be rewritten.

To break free from this cycle, we must learn to challenge the narratives we create. Ask yourself:

- **What am I telling myself about this situation?**

- **Is this story helpful or harmful?**

- **What evidence supports it, and what evidence contradicts it?**

By questioning the narrative, we loosen its grip and create space for new possibilities.

The Present Moment as Refuge

Fear thrives in the unknown future. But the present moment offers a refuge, a place where fear has no footing. In the present, there is no *"what if."* There is only *"what is."*

Maya found solace in this truth. She began practicing mindfulness, grounding herself in the here and now. When her thoughts drifted to fears of the future, she brought her focus back to her breath, the sensation of her feet on the ground, and the sounds outside her window. Slowly, she learned to trust that the present moment was enough.

In time, Maya found a new apartment, secured a better-paying job, and rebuilt her stability. However, the greatest transformation wasn't in her external circumstances, it was in her relationship with her thoughts. She had discovered a profound truth:

Pain and suffering don't come from what happens to us. Pain and suffering come from the stories we tell ourselves about what those events mean.

Once we learn to rewrite those stories, we reclaim our power. We remember that while we can't control the storms of life, we can choose how to weather them.

Chapter 4
There is Only Pain in The World

In the journey of leadership and life, pain is an inevitable companion. It's not a question of avoiding pain but deciding which type of pain you are willing to endure. Every decision, every action and every moment of inaction carries a cost. The cost is the pain of discipline or the pain of disappointment. This truth may seem stark, but it holds the key to living and leading with intention.

The Pain of Discipline

Discipline is the cornerstone of achievement. It's waking up early to prepare for the day ahead, putting in the hours to master a skill, and staying committed to your goals even when distractions and temptations arise. Discipline demands effort and sacrifice, but it rewards you with progress, growth and self-respect.

Deb was a young entrepreneur determined to launch her own business. Her evenings were spent creating business plans while her friends went out to unwind. Early mornings were filled with market research and customer calls. The discipline was grueling, but every small victory, a satisfied client, a successful pitch, reminded her why she chose this path. The pain of discipline gave her the joy of watching her dream come to life.

Discipline requires delayed gratification. It means saying no to what is easy now so you can achieve what is meaningful later. Having discipline is a marathon, not a sprint, and it requires a deep sense of purpose to keep going. But while the pain of discipline is real, so too are its rewards.

The Pain of Disappointment

Disappointment, on the other hand, is the cost of inaction, procrastination, or choosing comfort over growth. It is the sting of realizing you could have done more, worked harder or taken that opportunity when it was within reach. Unlike the pain of discipline, which often leads to fulfillment, the pain of disappointment leaves behind regret.

David, a talented musician who always dreamed of performing on stage, had the skills but lacked the discipline to practice consistently or seek out opportunities. As the years passed, he watched peers with less talent surpass him, achieving the success he had envisioned for himself. The pain of disappointment settled in, a quiet, persistent ache that whispered, "What if?"

The pain of disappointment often lingers longer than the pain of discipline. It eats away at confidence and builds a wall of self-doubt, making it harder to act in the future. While discipline empowers you, disappointment diminishes you.

The Leadership Perspective

As a leader, your choice between the pain of discipline or the pain of disappointment doesn't just affect you, it also affects those you lead. Discipline sets the standard, inspires your team, and creates a culture of accountability and resilience. Disappointment, on the other hand, erodes trust, morale and progress.

When leaders embrace discipline, they model perseverance. They show their teams that success is not about avoiding challenges but about confronting them head-on. A disciplined leader plans, executes and follows through, even when the road is tough. They build credibility and foster an environment where others feel safe to strive for excellence.

Conversely, a leader who succumbs to disappointment, who avoids hard decisions, fails to follow through or prioritizes short-term comfort over long-term goals, sends a message of complacency. Teams take their cues from their leaders, and a leader's disappointment can become the team's disappointment.

Practical Steps to Choose Discipline

1. **Define Your Why**: Discipline becomes easier when you have a clear sense of purpose. Ask yourself: Why does this matter? What's at stake if I don't follow through?

2. **Break It Down**: Big goals can feel overwhelming. Break them into manageable tasks and focus on one step at a time.

3. **Create Accountability**: Share your goals with someone you trust. Regular check-ins can keep you on track.

4. **Embrace the Process**: Discipline is a habit, not a one-time effort. Celebrate small wins and acknowledge your progress.

5. **Learn from Disappointment**: When you encounter disappointment, use it as a learning opportunity. What can you do differently next time?

Pain as a Choice

Life doesn't offer a pain-free path, but it does offer a choice. When you choose the pain of discipline, you take control of your journey. You accept the sacrifices necessary to achieve your goals and experience the fulfillment that comes with effort and growth.

When you avoid discipline, the pain of disappointment chooses you. It arrives unbidden, a reminder of missed opportunities and untapped potential. The choice is yours: endure the short-term discomfort of discipline or face the long-term regret of disappointment.

Great leaders understand this choice. They commit to discipline, not because it's easy, but because it's worth it. They choose growth over stagnation, action over inertia and progress over complacency. In doing so, they not only elevate themselves but also inspire those around them to rise to the challenge.

In the end, leadership is not about avoiding pain but about making it purposeful. Choose the pain that builds you, strengthens you and brings you closer to the life and legacy you envision. Choose discipline.

Chapter 5
The Irrational Desire for Control

In the realm of leadership, the temptation to control is strong. Control offers the illusion of certainty, the belief that by dictating outcomes and directing every move, we can guarantee success. But true power doesn't lie in control; it lies in influence. Influence is enduring, scalable, and deeply transformative; while control is often short-lived, rigid, and ultimately unsustainable.

The Illusion of Control

Control feels safe. It's the manager who insists on approving every decision, the leader who micromanages tasks, or the executive who imposes strict policies to minimize risk. But control has its limits. It stifles creativity, breeds resentment and creates bottlenecks. Worse, it can lead to disengagement as people lose their sense of ownership and autonomy.

Consider a team working under a controlling leader. Every decision must go through a single person, leaving little room for innovation or collaboration. Over time, team members stop offering ideas, knowing they'll likely be overruled. Productivity suffers and so does morale. The leader may feel in control, but their grip is ultimately a chokehold, stifling the team's potential.

The Enduring Power of Influence

Influence, on the other hand, is about guiding rather than directing. It's the ability to inspire, motivate, and empower others to act willingly. Unlike control, which relies on authority or fear, influence is rooted in trust, respect, and shared purpose.

A leader who prioritizes influence doesn't demand results; they inspire them. They create an environment where people want to contribute, not because they're obligated to, but because they believe in the mission and trust the leader's vision. Influence taps into intrinsic motivation, unlocking creativity, commitment and collaboration.

Influence in Action

Lisa was a director at a nonprofit organization. Her team was struggling to meet fundraising goals, and she knew she couldn't simply mandate success. Instead, she focused on building influence. She shared stories of the people their organization had helped, connecting the team to the mission. She listened to their ideas, encouraged experimentation and celebrated small wins.

As a result, her team felt empowered and motivated. They worked harder and smarter, not because Lisa controlled them, but because she inspired them. The team exceeded their goals, and their success felt shared, not imposed.

Why Influence Outlasts Control

1. **Sustainability**: Control relies on constant oversight, which is exhausting and impractical. Influence, however, builds momentum that continues even in the leader's absence.

2. **Scalability**: A controlling leader can only manage a limited number of people effectively. An influential leader, on the other hand, empowers others to lead, creating a ripple effect that extends far beyond their immediate reach.

3. **Adaptability**: Influence fosters a culture of trust and collaboration, making teams more resilient and adaptable.

When people feel valued and empowered, they're more willing to embrace change and take initiative.

4. **Legacy**: Control may achieve short-term results, but influence leaves a lasting impact. Influential leaders are remembered not for what they dictated but for what they inspired.

Building Influence

If influence is more powerful than control, how can leaders cultivate it? Here are some practical steps:

1. **Lead by Example**: Influence starts with integrity. Show up consistently, live your values and model the behaviors you want to see in others.

2. **Listen Actively**: Influence is a two-way street. Take the time to understand your team's perspectives, needs and ideas. People are more likely to follow someone who listens to them.

3. **Communicate a Vision**: Influence thrives on purpose. Share a clear, compelling vision that resonates with your team. Help them see how their work contributes to something bigger.

4. **Empower Others**: Trust your team to take ownership of their work. Provide guidance and support but give them the freedom to make decisions and learn from their experiences.

5. **Build Relationships**: Influence is rooted in trust and respect. Invest in building genuine connections with your

team. Show that you care about them as individuals, not just as employees.

6. **Celebrate Success**: Recognize and celebrate the contributions of others. Acknowledgment reinforces trust and motivation, strengthening your influence.

Influence as Leadership's True Measure

The measure of a leader is not how much they can control but how much they can inspire. Influence transforms teams into communities, ideas into movements and goals into achievements. It's the difference between compliance and commitment, between mediocrity and excellence.

Control may get results in the short term, but it comes at the cost of potential, trust and innovation. Influence, however, creates a foundation for sustained success. It's a force multiplier, enabling leaders to achieve far more than they ever could through control alone.

As you navigate your leadership journey, remember: the greatest leaders are not those who wield the most control but those who cultivate the most influence. By choosing influence, you choose to lead with purpose, to inspire others to rise to their potential, and to leave a legacy that endures.

Chapter 6
Trying May Lead to Failure But Failing to Try Will Guarantee It

"One day of a glorious life is worth more than a lifetime without a name."

- ***Thomas Osbert Mordaun***

"You are going to miss 100% of the shots you don't take."

- ***Wayne Gretzky***

At the end of it all, the true regret isn't failure, it's never stepping forward, never being known, never truly living. A lifetime spent in the background, avoiding risk and playing it safe, might be comfortable but it will never be extraordinary.

A single day filled with bold choices, deep connections and unforgettable experiences carries more weight than years spent merely existing. The world doesn't remember those who played it safe; it remembers those who took chances, made an impact and left their name behind.

The Fear That Keeps You Small

Many people live life as if they are avoiding loss rather than chasing gain. They hesitate to step forward, fearing judgment, failure or rejection. They stick to the familiar, believing it will protect them; but safety is an illusion, and the cost of playing small is far greater than the risk of going big.

What if you never take that shot?

What if you never introduce yourself to that person?

What if you never chase that opportunity?

At some point, the pain of wondering what could have been will outweigh the fear of taking the chance.

Your Name Is Your Legacy

You don't have to be famous to be remembered but you do have to be known. Whether in your career, your community or even just within your own family, your name should carry weight.

- Make people remember you, not for being loud, but for being impactful.

- Build relationships that matter, because opportunities don't come from resumes, they come from people.

- Stand for something, your values, your mission and your passion should be clear to everyone who meets you.

Every successful person you admire, leaders, innovators, artists, at some point decided to be known. They introduced themselves, took a bold step and built a network of people who believed in them.

Experience Over Comfort

The world is too big and too full of possibilities to be experienced from a single, safe place. You weren't meant to just survive, you were meant to experience.

- Travel, not just for fun, but to see how others live, how they think, how they work.

- Try new things, because every experience expands your perspective and your confidence.

- Say yes more often, even when it's scary, even when it's inconvenient, even when you don't feel ready.

Every great story you'll tell later comes from the moments you said yes when you could have said no.

The Power of Taking Chances

You don't build a legacy by waiting. You don't create an unforgettable life by staying in the background.

The people who make an impact, those who are remembered, step forward when most people hesitate. They raise their hand, take the job, introduce themselves and go after what they want.

Yes, taking chances means failing sometimes.

Yes, it means people will criticize you.

Yes, it means you'll be uncomfortable.

But what's the alternative? A lifetime of watching others live while you remain unseen?

One glorious day of stepping into the spotlight, making a bold move or experiencing something extraordinary is worth more than a lifetime of anonymity.

So go. Take the chance. Speak up. Make the connection. Say yes. Make sure that when your story is told, it's one worth remembering.

Chapter 7
Disasters of Unknown Benefit

Leadership is often romanticized as a seamless path of vision, strategy, and execution. But the truth is, leaders emerge, and are transformed, through adversity. Heroes are not born in comfort or ease; they rise when challenges and obstacles test their limits, stretch their capabilities and ignite their courage.

The Nature of Adversity

Obstacles are the crucibles in which heroes are forged. They are the fires that temper resolve, the storms that teach resilience and the trials that unveil latent strengths. Without obstacles, there is no growth, no transformation and no heroism.

Think of any great leader, from historical figures to modern-day innovators, their journeys are rarely linear. Instead, their journeys are marked by setbacks, failures and moments of doubt. It is precisely in those moments, however, that they find their true strength.

Consider Nelson Mandela, who faced 27 years of imprisonment under an oppressive regime. His struggle against apartheid was fraught with pain and loss, but it was in the face of those obstacles that his leadership crystallized. Mandela's heroism was not in avoiding hardship but in embracing it, using it to fuel his vision for a free and united South Africa.

Obstacles as Catalysts for Leadership

Obstacles are not roadblocks, they are steppingstones, and here is why they are essential to leadership development:

1. **They Build Resilience**: Leaders must learn to persevere in the face of adversity. Obstacles teach grit and the ability to bounce back stronger after every setback.

2. **They Clarify Purpose**: Challenges force leaders to reflect on their goals and priorities. When faced with adversity, a leader must ask: *"Why am I doing this? What truly matters?"*

3. **They Inspire Innovation**: Limitations breed creativity. When conventional paths are blocked, leaders must find new, uncharted ways forward.

4. **They Cultivate Empathy**: Experiencing hardship fosters a deeper understanding of others' struggles. Empathy is a cornerstone of effective leadership, and obstacles provide the perspective needed to connect with others authentically.

The Hero's Journey

Joseph Campbell's concept of the hero's journey provides a timeless framework for understanding how obstacles shape leaders. The journey begins with a call to adventure, often triggered by a challenge or crisis. Along the way, the hero faces trials, confronts fears and overcomes setbacks. These obstacles are not distractions, they are the essence of the journey, the moments that define the hero.

In leadership, the hero's journey might look like this:

- **The Call to Action**: A leader identifies a problem, a failing team, a societal injustice, or a market opportunity.

- **The Trials**: They face resistance, resource constraints and personal doubts.

- **The Transformation**: Through perseverance and adaptability, they emerge stronger, wiser and more capable.

- **The Return**: The leader brings newfound wisdom and success back to their team or community, inspiring others to rise.

Embracing Obstacles

If obstacles are the forge of heroism, how can leaders embrace them instead of avoiding them?

1. **Shift Your Mindset**: View challenges as opportunities for growth, not threats. Reframe obstacles as a necessary part of the journey.

2. **Lean Into Discomfort**: Growth lies at the edge of your comfort zone. Don't shy away from difficult conversations, tough decisions or uncertain paths.

3. **Cultivate Courage**: Courage is not the absence of fear but the willingness to act despite it. Trust in your ability to navigate adversity.

4. **Learn from Failure**: Every setback is a lesson. Analyze what went wrong, adapt and try again with newfound wisdom.

5. **Inspire Through Example**: When you face obstacles with determination, you inspire others to do the same. Your resilience becomes a beacon for your team.

Real-Life Heroes

History is replete with leaders who rose to greatness through adversity:

- **Abraham Lincoln**: Overcame repeated failures in business and politics before leading the United States through its most divisive period.

- **Oprah Winfrey**: Transformed a childhood of poverty and trauma into a platform for empowerment and global influence.

- **Temple Grandin**: An animal scientist and author who has inspired many through her challenges with autism and becoming a global leader in animal behavior research.

These heroes didn't avoid obstacles, they confronted them head-on, allowing the challenges to shape their character and define their legacy.

The Leader's Perspective

As a leader, obstacles are not your enemy, they are your greatest allies. They force you to adapt, innovate and grow. They reveal your true character and show your team what is possible when courage and determination take center stage.

Remember, leadership is not about having all the answers or an unbroken streak of successes. It's about rising after every fall, learning from every setback and inspiring others to do the same. Heroes are not those who avoid obstacles but those who use them as a springboard to greatness.

In the words of Marcus Aurelius, "The impediment to action advances action. What stands in the way becomes the way." Obstacles are not barriers, they are the path, and through them, heroes emerge.

Chapter 8
People Rarely Get To The Second Part Of Lombardi's Loser Quote

"Show me a good loser and I will show you a loser, but show me a gracious loser and I'll show you someone who will always be a winner." Vince Lombardi – Legendary NFL Head Coach

In leadership and in life, the most valuable lessons often come not from victory but from loss. Losing, though painful, is a profound teacher, a crucible where character is forged, resilience is built, and wisdom is gained. To win, you must first understand how to lose.

The Stigma of Losing

Our culture glorifies winners. The accolades go to the triumphant, the successful and the celebrated. But in this relentless pursuit of victory, losing is often vilified, seen as failure or inadequacy. This perspective, however, is shortsighted. Losing isn't the opposite of winning; it's an essential step on the journey to success. Great leaders know this. They embrace losing as an inevitable part of growth. For every public triumph, there are countless private defeats. What sets leaders apart is not the absence of loss but their ability to learn from it, adapt and come back stronger.

Lessons from Losing

1. **Humility**: Losing strips away ego and forces introspection. It reminds us that we are not infallible and that there is always room to grow.

2. **Resilience**: Every loss is an opportunity to build grit. It's easy to lead when things go well; the true test is how you respond when they don't.

3. **Perspective**: Losing puts things into context. It helps leaders focus on the bigger picture and prioritize what truly matters.

4. **Adaptability**: A loss often highlights blind spots or weaknesses. By addressing them, leaders become more adaptable and better prepared for future challenges.

Embracing the Learning Loser Mindset

To leverage the power of losing, leaders must adopt a mindset that views setbacks as steppingstones. Here's how:

1. **Own Your Losses**: Take responsibility for failures instead of blaming external factors. Ownership is the first step toward learning.

2. **Analyze Without Emotion**: Reflect on what went wrong with objectivity. Detach emotions from the analysis to focus on actionable insights.

3. **Seek Feedback**: Engage others to gain different perspectives on the loss. Constructive criticism can reveal lessons you might overlook.

4. **Commit to Growth**: Use every loss as an opportunity to improve. Set specific goals to address the gaps revealed by the setback.

5. **Celebrate the Effort**: Recognize the courage and effort it took to try. Celebrate the process, not just the outcome.

Stories of Learning Losers

- **Michael Jordan**: Widely regarded as one of the greatest basketball players of all time, Jordan famously said, "I've failed over and over and over again in my life. And that is why I succeed." His missed shots and lost games became the foundation for his relentless drive to improve.

- **Elite Tennis Players**: Top male players lose 40 – 45% of the points in a typical match. The ability to study the opponent and adjust throughout the match based on the players' strengths and the opponent's weaknesses allows them to come out as champions.

Turning Losing into Winning

1. **Reframe the Narrative**: Instead of seeing losses as failures, view them as experiments. Each loss is data that brings you closer to success.

2. **Normalize Losing**: Create a culture where setbacks are seen as part of the process. Encourage your team to take risks without fear of failure.

3. **Share Your Losses**: Vulnerability builds trust. By sharing your own losses, you inspire others to persevere through their own challenges.

4. **Prepare for the Next Challenge**: Apply what you've learned to future endeavors. Success isn't about avoiding losses, it's about losing better each time.

The Winning Formula

Winning starts with losing because losing teaches you what winning cannot. It reveals weaknesses, builds character, and sharpens focus. A leader who has never lost is a leader who has never truly been tested.

The path to greatness is paved with setbacks. By embracing the lessons of loss, you not only prepare for victory but also become a more empathetic, resilient and effective leader. So the next time you face a loss, don't despair, lean into it, learn from it and use it as a springboard to greater heights.

Chapter 9
Sometimes You Have to Move Forward
Without All The Facts

"Is today the day?" These were the words spoken by Sid Adsen, a radio operator and gunner in a B-24 bomber in World War II, to rally the troops as they prepared for D-Day. It was a reminder of the fleeting nature of life and the urgency of action. Even if we live long lives, the truth remains: life is short. We cannot predict the future, but we can decide how to act today, tomorrow and every day after that.

The Call to Action

The Commander's words weren't just about facing the enemy; they were about seizing the moment. In leadership, as in life, hesitation can be the enemy of progress. Every day presents opportunities to make a difference, but those opportunities are fleeting. What will you do today to ensure that you're moving forward, building momentum and creating impact?

Tomorrow's Weight

When we avoid action today, we carry its burden into tomorrow. Procrastination compounds challenges, making them harder to overcome. The tasks you avoided, the decisions you postponed and the risks you refused to take don't disappear, they accumulate. With more accumulation, the difficulty of moving forward also grows.

Ask yourself: How much harder will tomorrow be if you don't make today the day? Leaders must embrace the discipline of acting in the moment. The courage to tackle today's challenges lightens the load for the future.

Facing Uncertainty

Life is unpredictable. You could lose it all tomorrow: your job, your health or your opportunities. But even in the face of uncertainty, action remains the best course. If today isn't the day you achieve your ultimate goal, it can still be the day you make progress. By confronting challenges head-on, you grow stronger, wiser and more prepared for whatever comes next.

The alternative is to sit in the proverbial bunker, cowering in fear of what might happen. But how does that help? Avoiding the battle doesn't change the reality of the war. Leaders who shrink from action lose not only the chance to succeed but also the respect of those they lead.

Living the Question

"Is today the day?" is more than a motivational line, it's a guiding principle for leaders. Every morning, ask yourself:

1. **What can I do today to make a difference?** Identify one action, however small, that moves you closer to your goals.

2. **What am I avoiding?** Confront the tasks or decisions you've been putting off.

3. **How will today's actions shape tomorrow?** Consider the long-term impact of what you do, or don't do, today.

The Power of Momentum

Action creates momentum. Even small victories build confidence and set the stage for bigger successes. By choosing to act today, you set a precedent for tomorrow. You train yourself and your team to face challenges head-on, to prioritize progress over perfection and to value action over hesitation.

The Leader's Choice

As a leader, your actions set the tone for those around you. If you lead with urgency and purpose, your team will follow. If you hesitate, so will your team. Leadership is about more than making decisions; it's about inspiring others to act.

Life is short. You may not know what tomorrow holds, but you do know what today offers: a chance to make an impact, to grow and to lead. So, is today the day? That's a question only you can answer. But remember, the cost of inaction is far greater than the risk of trying.

Chapter 10
The Art of Facilitating the Retreat

The ancient wisdom of Sun Tzu's *Art of War* reminds us of a fundamental truth in conflict resolution: "Pave your enemies a bridge of gold onto which they can retreat." This metaphorical bridge is not an act of charity or weakness but a strategic move that benefits all parties involved. It recognizes the human need for dignity and the importance of creating an exit strategy that allows opponents to save face.

The Power of Saving Face

Conflict often pushes people into corners where they feel they must fight to the bitter end to preserve their pride or reputation. In these moments, logic and reason are often overshadowed by emotion and ego. Leaders who understand this dynamic wield a powerful tool: the ability to offer an honorable way out.

By giving your adversary a path that feels like a win, you defuse tension and create a resolution that minimizes damage. When retreat is presented as a viable option, even one that offers an advantage, it becomes easier for the other party to choose it without feeling like they've lost.

A Lesson from Harry Truman

President Harry Truman understood the concept of "building a bridge of gold onto which they can retreat very well." When he needed to remove someone from a position, he famously prepared two letters. The first letter praised the individual, highlighting their contributions and framing the transition as an honorable one. The second letter, however, carried the weight of potential investigations and consequences, serving as a stern reminder of the stakes.

The choice was clear: take the golden bridge of the first letter, preserving dignity and reputation, or face the harsher realities outlined in the second. Truman's approach was both pragmatic and compassionate, giving his adversaries a way to retreat without unnecessary conflict.

When Someone Feels Conquered, They Will Eventually Rebel

Throughout history, we have seen leaders dominate constituents and enemies and overpower them with force and dominance. However, the people who were dominated do not stay down forever. They will eventually rebel and fight, even to the death. Overpowering someone creates a mental position that causes an emotion to lash out and fight back even harder and at times without fear of personal loss.

Building the Bridge

1. **Recognize the Stakes**: Understand what your opponent values most. Is it their reputation? Their position? Their relationships? Build the bridge around what they're most motivated to protect.

2. **Frame Retreat as a Win**: Present the path you're offering not as a concession but as an opportunity. Highlight the benefits of taking this path and how it aligns with their interests.

3. **Communicate Respect**: Even in conflict, respect is essential. By demonstrating empathy and understanding, you increase the likelihood of your bridge being accepted.

4. **Be Prepared for Resistance**: Not everyone will take the bridge immediately. Patience and persistence are key. Keep the door open and the bridge sturdy.

The Golden Bridge in Leadership

In leadership, this principle extends beyond conflict resolution. It applies to managing change, navigating difficult conversations and fostering collaboration. When people feel backed into a corner, they resist. But when they see an honorable way forward, they engage.

Whether you're negotiating a high-stakes deal, mediating a dispute, or guiding your team through a challenging transition, remember the power of the golden bridge. Give others a way to save face, and you'll not only resolve the immediate conflict but also build trust and goodwill for the future.

A Bridge to Better Leadership

True leadership is not about winning at all costs. It's about achieving outcomes that move everyone forward. The golden bridge is a symbol of this ethos, a reminder that dignity, respect and strategy are not mutually exclusive. By paving the way for others to retreat honorably, you pave the way for your own success.

Chapter 11
The Middle Of The Road Sounds Good Until You Hear The Traffic Coming

Former United States Secretary of State George P Schultz commented on being indecisive in conflict with the statement, "He who walks in the middle of the road gets hit from both sides."

Leadership is not about pleasing everyone. As a leader, one of the most challenging truths you will face is this: at some point, you must pick a side. Attempting to balance on the metaphorical median of the road often leads to one inevitable outcome: getting hit from both sides.

The Danger of Indecision

Imagine trying to navigate a busy intersection by standing in the middle of the road, hesitant to commit to a direction. Cars speed by on either side, horns blaring, as you find yourself paralyzed by the fear of choosing wrong. The longer you stand there, the more vulnerable you become. This is the reality for leaders who try to make everyone happy.

In leadership, as in life, the pursuit of universal approval is a fool's errand. When you expend your energy trying to satisfy every stakeholder, every team member, and every critic, you deplete yourself. Worse yet, you accomplish little of value. Instead of uniting your team or organization, you fracture it. Disappointment becomes inevitable, and the unhappiness you feared spreads to everyone, yourself included.

Picking a Side: Integrity, Culture, and Priorities

Leadership requires clarity of values and the courage to stand by them. As the old adage goes, if you don't stand for something, you will fall for anything. Integrity, culture and a focus on what truly matters must guide your decisions. These elements become your compass, helping you navigate the complexities of leadership with confidence and purpose.

Integrity is non-negotiable. It is the foundation of trust, the bedrock of your leadership. When you choose integrity, you choose to act in alignment with your values, even when it is inconvenient or unpopular. Leaders who compromise their integrity in an attempt to please everyone ultimately lose the respect of those they lead.

Culture is another critical consideration. As a leader, you are the steward of your organization's culture. Every decision you make either reinforces or undermines the values and norms you wish to uphold. Picking a side means advocating for a culture that aligns with your organization's mission and vision. It means setting the tone for how people treat one another, how they approach challenges and how they celebrate success.

Finally, **prioritization** is key. Not all issues are created equal, and not all battles are worth fighting. Picking a side doesn't mean being inflexible or combative, it means focusing your energy on what matters most. Identify the goals and principles that are non-negotiable and let them guide your decisions. When you lead with a clear sense of purpose, you inspire others to follow.

The Myth of the Balancing Act

One of the most pervasive misconceptions about leadership is the idea that it is a balancing act, that great leaders somehow manage to be all things to all people. This is a myth. Leadership is not about balance; it is about alignment.

Trying to be all things to all people is like trying to balance on a tightrope while juggling flaming torches. It's unsustainable and, ultimately, counterproductive. Instead of striving for balance, focus on alignment. Align your actions with your values, your vision, and your goals. Align your team's efforts with the organization's mission. When alignment replaces balance, clarity replaces confusion and purpose replaces chaos.

Leadership Takeaway

The road to effective leadership is not paved with compromises and concessions; it is marked by conviction and courage. To lead is to choose, to pick a side and stand firmly by it. Yes, this may mean disappointing some people or facing criticism. But it also means earning the respect and trust of those who share your vision.

So, step off the median. Choose integrity over expediency. Choose culture over convenience. Choose priorities over popularity. By doing so, you will not only protect yourself from being hit from both sides, but you will also pave the way for meaningful progress and lasting impact.

Chapter 12
The Idea of It vs. The Reality of It

Life often begins with enticing dreams. The idea of pursuing something new, whether it's a career move, a relationship or a major purchase, sounds thrilling, even glamorous. But much like owning a swimming pool, the reality can be far more complex, requiring effort, commitment and a sobering reckoning with hidden costs.

The Seduction of the Idea

The initial allure of a big decision is powerful. It's easy to picture the rewards: the happiness it will bring, the opportunities it will create, the fulfillment it promises. Pursuing your dreams seems like a no-brainer, a chance to create the life you've always imagined.

This vision of pursuing your dreams is not inherently wrong. Big decisions and bold moves can lead to incredible personal growth. However, the idea of something often glosses over the less glamorous truths: the sacrifices, the hard work and the reality of what it truly takes to succeed.

Consider the metaphor of a swimming pool. When you first dream of owning one, you envision summer afternoons spent lounging by the water, hosting pool parties and enjoying serene morning swims. The cost seems justifiable when weighed against these idyllic images, but how often do you really use it? And how much effort and money does it take to maintain it? It becomes very painful to learn the cost per hour if you are swimming three times per year. Life decisions, like that swimming pool, come with a price.

The Reality: The Idea of It vs The Reality of It

One of the most important skills in leadership, and in life, is the ability to separate the idea of something from the reality of it. It's easy to fall in love with an exciting vision, a bold initiative, or a new opportunity. The idea of it is often perfect, clean and full of potential; it's where dreams are made.

The reality of it is something else entirely. Reality comes with trade-offs, costs, complications and unforeseen challenges. Successful leaders develop the ability to see past the initial excitement and analyze whether an idea will actually work, not just in theory, but in practice.

The Gap Between Perception and Reality

Many poor decisions, both personal and professional, come from failing to close the gap between what we think something will be and what it actually is. Consider the following:

- A business owner invests in flashy new technology, only to realize later that adoption is low and it creates more problems than it solves.

- A company hires a highly sought-after executive, expecting them to revolutionize the business, but they struggle to adapt to the existing culture.

- An entrepreneur expands too quickly, only to find that the costs of scaling outweigh the revenue growth.

- A leader commits to a massive rebranding effort, assuming it will improve the company's image, but it alienates existing customers and causes confusion.

These are all examples of decisions made on the idea of something rather than its reality.

How to Analyze the Idea vs. the Reality

Before making a major decision, strong leaders ask key questions to determine whether an idea is truly worth pursuing:

1. What is the actual problem we are solving?

- Is this a real need or just a nice-to-have?

- Are we reacting to a trend or addressing a fundamental issue?

- Will this idea create a meaningful impact or just look good on paper?

2. What are the hidden costs: time, money, and energy?

- Many ideas look simple but their execution is anything but.

- Who will maintain this? Who will be responsible for making it work?

- What other priorities will be sacrificed if we commit to this?

3. What are the long-term consequences?

- Will this decision limit our flexibility in the future?

- Could this become a burden rather than an asset?

- If this doesn't work as expected, how easy is it to walk away?

4. Who benefits from this and who is responsible when it fails?

- Is this idea truly valuable or is someone just selling us on it?

- Are we doing this because it aligns with our vision or because it looks good to outsiders?

- If this doesn't succeed, who absorbs the cost?

5. Have we tested this in a small way before committing?

- Can we pilot it before fully investing?

- Have we studied others who have tried this and learned from their mistakes?

- What is the minimum viable version of this idea that allows us to see its true potential?

The Discipline to Say No

The best leaders don't just see reality clearly, they also have the discipline to say no when an idea doesn't hold up under scrutiny.

- They don't chase every new opportunity just because it's exciting.

- They don't get caught up in what looks good on the surface without considering the deeper implications.

- They know that the best decision is sometimes to walk away.

Great decision-making isn't about rejecting big ideas; it's about pursuing the right ones. The ability to separate the idea of something from the reality of it is what ensures that time, energy and resources are invested wisely.

Because in the end, success doesn't come from chasing what seems great in theory, it comes from choosing what actually works in practice.

Chapter 13
The Winner in Life Has the Fewest Keys

The wealthiest people don't have car keys because they have a driver, and they don't have a house key because they have a doorman, and they don't have a key to the office because someone else opens and closes the office.

In the pursuit of personal success, we often equate accomplishment with accumulation: more assets, more responsibilities, more tools. But what if the true measure of freedom and success isn't about how much you have, but how little you need? What if the man with the fewest keys truly wins?

Keys as a Metaphor

Keys, both literal and figurative, represent responsibility. They are the means by which we access and control the various elements of our lives. A car key enables us to drive, an office key grants us entry to our workspace, and the keys we hold in our mind, metaphors for tasks, obligations, and roles, define how we spend our time and energy.

The problem with keys is that they bind us. Each key we carry, whether physical or metaphorical, is a reminder of something we must manage, maintain or oversee. The more keys we have, the less freedom we enjoy. True success, then, lies in eliminating the unnecessary keys in our lives, freeing ourselves to focus on what truly matters.

The Cost of Carrying Keys

Imagine a keyring heavy with dozens of keys. Each key serves a purpose, but together, they become a burden. In life, these keys take many forms: responsibilities we could delegate, tasks that don't align with our talents and possessions that demand our attention but offer little in return.

1. Wasted Energy:

Every key you carry requires mental and physical effort. Whether it's the car you maintain, the office space you manage, or the mundane tasks you perform; each key drains energy that could be better spent elsewhere.

2. Limited Focus:

The more keys you carry, the harder it is to focus on what truly matters. Your time and attention are finite resources. When they're divided among too many responsibilities, your effectiveness suffers.

3. Lost Freedom:

Every key represents something tying you down. The man with the most keys is not free, he is burdened. Freedom comes not from owning and controlling more, but from needing and managing less.

Eliminating the Keys

So how do we lighten the load? How do we become the man with the fewest keys? The answer lies in reevaluating what's truly necessary and embracing the power of delegation, automation, and simplification.

1. Delegate:

Not every task requires your personal attention. If you have the resources, delegate responsibilities that don't align with your highest and best use of time and talent. Hire a driver instead of carrying a car key. Employ a personal assistant to manage your schedule. Trust capable individuals to handle the tasks that don't require your unique skills.

2. Simplify:

Examine your life for unnecessary complexity. Do you really need an office key if your work can be done remotely? Do you need a large home with multiple locks, or would a simpler space better serve your needs? By simplifying your environment and your commitments, you reduce the keys you carry both physically and metaphorically.

3. Automate:

In the modern age, technology offers countless opportunities to automate repetitive tasks. From smart locks to automated billing systems, leverage tools that eliminate the need for manual effort. Automation allows you to focus on what truly matters while the background processes take care of themselves.

Keys and Talent

At its core, the philosophy of "fewer keys" is about aligning your life with your highest and best use of talent. Every key you carry that doesn't serve this purpose is a distraction. The more keys you shed, the more time and energy you have to focus on what you do best and what brings you the greatest fulfillment.

Freedom doesn't come from having the resources to carry more keys; it comes from the wisdom to carry fewer. By eliminating unnecessary responsibilities and focusing on your strengths, you unlock a life of greater purpose and clarity.

Leadership Takeaway

The man with the fewest keys wins because he understands that success is not about accumulation but liberation. He chooses to focus on what truly matters, delegating, simplifying and automating the rest. In doing so, he gains the ultimate prize: freedom.

So, take a look at the keys you carry. Which ones truly serve you? Which ones could you let go? By lightening your load, you take one step closer to a life of purpose, clarity, and unparalleled success.

Chapter 14
The Benevolent Dictator: A Model for Entrepreneurial Leadership

When we think of leadership styles, the term "dictator" might raise eyebrows. It conjures images of control, rigidity and fear. However, when paired with the word "benevolent," it assumes a transformative meaning, particularly in the context of entrepreneurship. The "benevolent dictator" is a leader who wields authority not for personal gain but for the collective good. This leadership style, when executed thoughtfully, can drive extraordinary success in entrepreneurial ventures.

What is a Benevolent Dictator?

A benevolent dictator is a leader who exercises strong, centralized authority while maintaining an unwavering commitment to the welfare of their team, organization and mission. Unlike authoritarian leaders who demand compliance through fear, benevolent dictators earn loyalty through trust, respect and the consistent demonstration of care for their people.

This model is particularly effective in entrepreneurial environments where speed, decisiveness and vision are critical. Startups and growing businesses often operate in fast moving, high-stakes markets where consensus-driven decision making can lead to delays and missed opportunities. A benevolent dictator cuts through the noise, making decisions swiftly and confidently while ensuring that those decisions serve the greater good.

The Key Principles of Benevolent Dictatorship

To successfully embody this leadership style, an entrepreneur must balance authority with empathy. The following principles are key:

1. Clarity:

A benevolent dictator must have a clear and compelling vision for their organization. This vision serves as the guiding star for decision-making and inspires the team to rally behind a common goal. Clarity of vision eliminates confusion and fosters alignment, enabling the leader to act decisively without constant second-guessing. This vision, as well as culture, client experience, employee experience and the values of the company must be clearly communicated to all stakeholders. Clear communication allows people to run full speed without fear and excel in their role.

2. Trust Through Transparency:

Authority without trust breeds resentment. A benevolent dictator earns trust by being transparent about their intentions, decisions and the reasoning behind them. This openness demonstrates respect for the team's intelligence and reinforces the leader's commitment to shared success.

3. Empathy in Action:

Benevolence is not about words, it's about actions. A benevolent dictator consistently demonstrates care for their team's well-being, both professionally and personally. They understand the challenges their employees face and take steps to address them, whether through fair compensation, work-life balance initiatives or opportunities for growth.

4. Decisive Leadership with Active Listening, Collaboration and Personal Responsibility for Results:

In entrepreneurial settings, indecision can be fatal. A benevolent dictator embraces their role as the ultimate decision-maker, taking responsibility for making tough calls and accepting the consequences. Their decisiveness keeps the organization agile and forward moving.

A benevolent dictator creates an environment of collaboration and inclusion. Gaining buy-in from listening to colleagues and understanding perspectives from all stakeholders of the business. They ask questions and listen to seek understanding of realities that exist in every aspect of the business. However, they realize that democratic models of everyone voting for decisions turn into slow and diluted outcomes. So, after listening, collaborating and including people in how to execute, they make decisions with conviction and take full responsibility for the outcomes.

5. Accountability:

With great authority comes great responsibility. A benevolent dictator holds themselves accountable for the outcomes of their decisions. They do not deflect blame onto others but instead use failures as opportunities to learn and grow. This accountability fosters a culture of mutual respect and shared ownership.

Why This Model Works for Entrepreneurs

Entrepreneurial ventures thrive on speed, innovation and adaptability. The benevolent dictator model aligns perfectly with these demands for several reasons:

1. Agility in Decision-Making:

Startups and growing businesses operate in dynamic environments where hesitation can mean losing a competitive edge. A benevolent dictator's ability to make swift, informed decisions ensures that the organization remains proactive rather than reactive.

2. Unified Direction:

When everyone understands and trusts the leader's vision, the organization moves in unison. This alignment minimizes internal friction and maximizes the team's collective energy.

3. Cultivation of Loyalty:

Teams are more likely to stay engaged and committed when they feel valued and cared for. Benevolent dictators cultivate loyalty by prioritizing the needs of their employees and fostering a sense of purpose.

4. Resilience in Uncertainty:

Entrepreneurship is fraught with uncertainty. A benevolent dictator's confidence and steadiness provide a sense of stability, even in turbulent times. This resilience inspires the team to persevere through challenges.

The Potential Pitfalls and How to Avoid Them

While the benevolent dictator model has its advantages, it also carries risks if not carefully managed:

1. Overreach:

Exercising too much control can stifle creativity and innovation. A benevolent dictator must know when to step back and empower others to contribute their ideas and expertise.

2. Misinterpretation of Intentions:

Even well-meaning decisions can be perceived as self-serving if not communicated effectively. Transparency and consistent actions are essential to maintaining trust.

3. Burnout:

The responsibility of being the sole decision maker can be exhausting. To avoid burnout, a benevolent dictator should build a trusted inner circle of advisors and delegate tasks when appropriate.

Leadership Takeaway

The benevolent dictator model is not about wielding unchecked power; it's about leading with authority, empathy and purpose. For entrepreneurs, this leadership style offers a way to navigate the complexities of building and scaling a business with clarity, decisiveness and care.

To be a benevolent dictator is to accept the weight of leadership with grace and humility. It is to make tough decisions for the benefit of the whole, to inspire trust through transparency and action, and to lead with both strength and compassion. In doing so, you create not just a successful business but a legacy of leadership that others will seek to emulate.

Chapter 15
The Gold Miner's Paradox:
Don't Get Eaten by the Bear

The Illusion of Accumulation

Imagine yourself deep in the Yukon, knee-deep in an icy river, panning for gold. You've spent weeks, maybe months, tirelessly searching, and finally, you strike it rich. Nugget by nugget, you begin accumulating wealth. The thrill of discovery fuels you, and soon, you have a stash big enough to change your life.

But here's the problem: Gold in the wilderness is worthless.

It can't buy you food, shelter, or safety. It's just metal in your pocket. It only becomes valuable when you convert it into something useful, whether that's trading it for goods, securing your future, or creating experiences that enrich your life.

Many miners in history never made it that far. They died with their gold still clutched in their hands, killed by the wilderness, robbed by desperate thieves or simply too consumed by the chase to ever stop and use what they found. This is the Gold Miner's Paradox, the mistaken belief that accumulation is the whole game, when in reality, it's only the first step.

The Three Phases of True Wealth

Accumulation: The Pursuit of Resources

- In life, we all start by accumulating, whether it's wealth, knowledge, skills or relationships.

- Hard work, persistence and discipline allow us to gather resources.

- Too many people stop with accumulation, thinking more is always better.

Conversion: Turning Resources into Real Value

- Gold must be converted to be useful. In life, this means translating wealth into security, knowledge into wisdom and relationships into opportunities.

- Many fail at this step, hoarding what they've collected instead of transforming it into something meaningful.

- A miner who never cashes in dies rich in theory but poor in reality.

Deployment: Using Wealth for Impact & Fulfillment

- The final step is deployment, putting what you've earned into action.

- This could mean investing in a home, giving to charity, creating joy for yourself and others, or taking risks to grow even further.

- True leaders understand that wealth, whether financial, intellectual, or social, is only valuable when it is used.

The Danger of Hoarding Without Purpose

Many people spend their entire lives accumulating money, titles, possessions, only to realize too late that they never converted or deployed it.

- The executive who chases promotions but never builds a life outside of work.

- The entrepreneur who earns millions but never enjoys time with family.

- The investor who hoards cash but is too afraid to take risks or give back.

Like the miners who died with gold in their pockets, they focused too much on getting more and not enough on what it was for.

Living Beyond the Paradox

To escape the Gold Miner's Paradox, you must constantly ask yourself:

- What am I accumulating and why?

- How can I convert what I have into something valuable?

- Am I deploying my resources in a way that truly benefits me and others?

Wealth, knowledge and relationships are all tools. If they are never used, they are meaningless. The most successful and fulfilled people are not just great accumulators; they are masters of conversion and deployment. They understand that gold is not the prize, it's just the beginning. So, don't just gather. Don't just hold. Use. Move. Deploy. That's where real wealth is found.

Chapter 16
Three Things to Do with Money: Necessity, Luxury, and Charity.

Money is one of life's most misunderstood and mismanaged resources. It shapes lives, creates opportunities and often defines legacies. Despite its central role, few approach money with intentionality. A clear, guiding principle can profoundly transform one's financial and emotional health. Embracing the concept that money serves three fundamental purposes, necessity, luxury, and charity, provides clarity and intention, shaping our personal leadership and life skills.

Necessity: The Foundation of Stability

Necessity covers the basics: food, shelter, clothing, healthcare and education. These are not mere preferences, they are foundational elements essential to survival and personal dignity. Meeting these needs should always take precedence. A secure foundation allows us to focus our energies on growth, contribution and the enjoyment of life without constant fear or anxiety.

Leaders and successful individuals who overlook or underestimate the importance of necessity do so at their peril. Neglecting fundamental security to pursue short-term luxury can lead to profound instability, derailing long-term goals. Effective leaders prioritize necessities, ensuring resilience and a stable platform for themselves and those who depend on them.

Luxury: The Joyful Celebration of Success

Luxury is everything we desire beyond necessity. It isn't about needs; it's about desires, aspirations and celebrations of success. Luxury manifests differently for everyone; it might be travel, a beautiful home, fine dining or a new sports car.

Luxuries are not inherently selfish or irresponsible; they are rewards and reflections of achievement. They remind us that life is not just about survival but also about thriving, experiencing joy and savoring successes.

Yet, understanding luxury also demands wisdom. While luxury enhances life, unchecked indulgence can lead to emptiness or financial ruin. Leaders skilled in the isms of life recognize luxury as a measured, conscious celebration. They understand that prudent enjoyment of luxuries is an art, one balanced with ongoing responsibility and self-awareness.

A powerful insight here is captured in the saying, "If you don't fly first class, your children will." It's a stark reminder that enjoyment deferred indefinitely only benefits others, often those who might not appreciate the sacrifices made to accumulate wealth.

Charity: Leaving a Meaningful Legacy

Charity encompasses the generosity we show toward others, driven by a recognition that we will not take anything with us. Our true to-go box is our coffin. Every dollar we hold will eventually be released to someone or something else, children, community organizations or charitable causes. Accumulating wealth without a clear deployment plan merely postpones difficult decisions, frequently resulting in family discord or misused legacies.

Effective leaders don't just accumulate resources; they thoughtfully deploy them. Charitable giving is not only morally uplifting, but it also reinforces empathy, builds community and fosters gratitude. Leaders who integrate charity as a core strategy are remembered not for their bank balance but for the impact and legacy of their generosity.

The uncomfortable reality remains: What you don't want on your tombstone is that you worked tirelessly for the benefit of your heirs. Effective planning ensures wealth becomes a source of empowerment rather than contention or regret. Open communication, clearly articulated intentions, and strategic charitable contributions help preserve harmony and ensure the legacy is positive and purposeful.

Integrated Financial Wisdom

Balancing Necessity, Luxury and Charity provides an integrated approach to wealth management, leadership and personal satisfaction. Leaders must ensure their resources effectively support their foundational needs, provide joyful and meaningful celebrations of success, and allow them to leave an impactful legacy.

Ultimately, money should serve our lives, not dominate them. By deliberately balancing necessity, luxury and charity, leaders and individuals can align their financial actions with their deepest values and leave a legacy that is thoughtful, meaningful and truly impactful.

Chapter 17
Buzzard Life – The Lifestyle
Brand of Leadership

The Eagle vs The Buzzard

Leadership has long been associated with the majestic eagle, soaring high, strong, proud and always admired. Eagles are revered, honored and used as symbols of greatness. Their image graces coins, flags and statues. But the true essence of leadership isn't found in the eagle; it's found in the buzzard.

The Unflappable Nature of the Buzzard

A buzzard does what others refuse to do. It cleans up the mess, removes the filth, and does the unglamorous work that keeps the ecosystem in balance. You can't make a buzzard "throw up" because it's born with an unshakable purpose. You also can't disappoint a buzzard because it doesn't seek admiration or approval. It doesn't get grossed out or thrown off its game. It simply does what it is designed to do, day in and day out, without complaint and without recognition.

Unlike eagles, buzzards aren't given medals or immortalized in symbols of power. Eagles hunt for themselves, securing fresh meat and looking out for their own survival. Buzzards take care of the community, ensuring that roads are cleared and decay is managed. They eat the three-day-old opossum that no one else will touch, and they do it without expecting a thank you.

The Peace of Being a Buzzard

As a leader, you will find that no one will give you credit for the work you do, and that's exactly where peace begins. If you are constantly seeking recognition, if you expect gratitude, you are setting yourself up for disappointment. True leadership is about embracing the buzzard life, not seeking the spotlight but ensuring that the work gets done even when it's thankless, even when it's unpleasant.

If you eat fresh meat, that is for you. If you eat what the buzzard eats, you build the resilience necessary to withstand the realities of leadership. It is in this mindset that you learn how to handle disappointment, how to endure when followers are selfish or ungrateful, and how to persevere in the face of an unending supply of setbacks. The irrational right of control does not exist for a leader. People will do what they want and choose to do, and you must continue leading regardless.

Sacrificial Leadership: Beyond Servant Leadership

The term *servant leadership* is overused and often misunderstood. The problem with servant leadership is that it still allows room for serving yourself. True leadership, *sacrificial leadership*, is selfless. A sacrificial leader doesn't prioritize their own interests. They are willing to step aside if someone else is better suited for the role. They don't lead for personal gain, admiration or control. They lead because the work must be done and they are willing to do it even if it means sacrificing comfort, recognition and self-interest.

To lead like a buzzard is to embrace the hard, unglamorous work of leadership. It means doing what others avoid. It means not being rattled by ungrateful followers. It means finding peace in knowing that leadership is about service, sacrifice and an unwavering commitment to the mission, whether anyone recognizes it or not.

Eagles may soar, but buzzards sustain, and that is the true essence of leadership.

Chapter 18
Your Position and Your Ego, May the Two Never Meet

Never Put Your Position So Close to Your Ego That When Your Position Fails, Your Ego Goes with It

Leadership is not just about holding a position, it's about understanding that positions are temporary, but character and impact are lasting. Many leaders make the mistake of intertwining their identity with their title. They believe that their worth is defined by their rank, their office or their authority. But when that position is taken away, changed or lost, their confidence and self-worth crumble with it. This is a dangerous trap.

The Illusion of Permanence

Leadership positions are fleeting. Whether you are a CEO, a manager, a coach or a community leader, the truth remains: You will not always hold that title. If your ego is too closely tied to your position, its loss will feel like a personal failure rather than a natural transition. Leaders who make their position their identity often react poorly to challenges, changes and criticisms because they see these as direct attacks on their self-worth rather than opportunities for growth.

Baby boomers, in particular, tend to attach their personal value to what they do for a living and what they own. This mindset can be dangerous because it makes it incredibly difficult to ever leave a job.

When self-worth is defined by a paycheck, a title or material possessions, stepping away from a career feels like losing one's identity. This leads to leaders holding onto positions longer than they should, sometimes to the detriment of both themselves and the organizations they serve.

Leading Without Attachment

The most effective leaders understand that their role is a responsibility, not an entitlement. Their goal is to serve, guide, and influence, not to seek validation from the title they hold. When you separate your ego from your position, you:

- Lead with humility rather than arrogance.

- Make better decisions based on what is right rather than what protects your status.

- Handle transitions and setbacks with grace and resilience.

- Stay open to feedback and growth rather than becoming defensive.

When Positions Fail

Every leader will experience setbacks. A promotion that never comes. A restructuring that eliminates your role. A company that doesn't survive market changes. If your identity is wrapped up in your title, these events will feel devastating. But if you've built your foundation on character rather than status, you will be able to move forward with confidence.

The best leaders see their positions as platforms for service, not as sources of self-worth. They understand that leadership is about making an impact, not securing a pedestal. If you lose a role but maintain your integrity, wisdom and relationships, you have lost nothing of true value.

True Leadership is Beyond Titles

A title may give you authority, but it does not make you a leader. Influence, respect and legacy are earned through actions, not through rank. Leadership is about how you treat people, how you make decisions and how you handle adversity. If you lead well, people will follow you regardless of your title.

Never allow your position to define who you are. Instead, focus on the qualities that make you a great leader, your wisdom, your integrity and your ability to inspire others. When you do this, you will never fear losing a title, because you will know that your leadership is built on something far greater than a position, it is built on character.

Chapter 19
Our Only Real Choices in Life –
Embrace & Endure

Life and leadership require discipline, hard work and perseverance. In these moments, you have two choices: embrace the challenge or simply endure it.

To embrace the challenge is to recognize that the difficulty itself is the pathway to growth. It's an understanding that, while it will be tough, it is shaping you into something stronger. When you embrace, you say, *This is going to be hard, but I know it is getting me where I need to go.* It becomes an exercise of embracing what is difficult to do, knowing the other side has great potential of joy, success, and accomplishment.

Enduring the challenge, on the other hand, is about suffering through the difficulty, counting down the moments until it's over. When you endure, you focus on how bad things are, wishing it away rather than extracting its benefits.

Connecting the Dots: If You Hate It, It Won't Last

Think of any demanding discipline, exercise, leadership or skill development. If you truly hate the process, it won't last, you will eventually quit. But if you can connect the dots between the challenge and its long-term benefits, you can shift from enduring to embracing. The clearer the value, the more likely you are to embrace rather than simply tolerate the struggle.

A competitive bike racer used to see climbing as a necessary evil, an exhausting and grueling part of his training. Every steep incline felt like punishment. He endured it because he had to, but he dreaded every moment.

Then, one day, he reframed his mindset. He realized that every hill he climbed in training was making him stronger for race day. Instead of seeing climbs as suffering, he started seeing them as opportunities. He attacked the hills with energy, knowing that each painful ascent was a deposit into his future success.

By shifting his mindset from endurance to embrace, he found more energy, enthusiasm and motivation in his training. The task itself didn't change, his perspective did.

The Chemistry of Mindset

Your brain releases chemicals based on how you approach a challenge. When you embrace a difficult task, your body responds by releasing dopamine, a neurotransmitter that enhances motivation and focus. Your brain rewards you for seeing the challenge as an opportunity.

However, when you endure, viewing a task as suffering, your body triggers stress hormones like cortisol, which prepares you for survival rather than peak performance. Your body sees the situation as a threat rather than an opportunity, making the experience feel even worse.

By choosing to embrace instead of endure, you set yourself up for success not only mentally but chemically. You unlock a biological advantage that allows you to push further, work harder and stay engaged longer.

The Shift to Embrace

The difference between success and stagnation is often just a mindset shift. Do you see challenges as obstacles or as steppingstones? The most resilient leaders and performers don't just survive difficult situations, they lean into them with purpose.

When you embrace, you seek out opportunities for growth rather than looking for an escape. You transform hardship into an advantage. The road ahead will be difficult, but the choice is yours: suffer through it or embrace it and thrive.

Chapter 20
Two Types of People

Two types of people: Those who have what they want and want to protect it, and those who don't have what they want and cause disruption to get it.

In leadership, business and life, people generally fall into two categories: those who are satisfied with what they have and focus on protecting it, and those who are dissatisfied and willing to disrupt the status quo to get what they desire. Understanding these two types is critical for predicting behavior, making strategic decisions and leading effectively.

The Cave Dweller vs. The Desert Wanderer

Imagine two men. One lives in a cave by a freshwater stream, surrounded by fertile land and abundant resources. He has everything he needs to survive, food, water, shelter, and stability. His primary concern is protecting what he has. He fortifies his cave, guards his resources and avoids unnecessary risks that could jeopardize his comfort.

The other man lives in a desert and struggles against harsh conditions. He lacks water, food is scarce and survival is a constant battle. He cannot afford to sit still and protect what little he has because what he has is not enough. His only option is to disrupt. He must seek new opportunities, challenge those who have resources and shift the balance of power to secure a better life.

The cave dweller is playing defense, the desert wanderer is playing offense. The cave dweller is protecting, the desert wanderer is attacking. The cave dweller is focused on maintaining the desert wanderer is focused on advancing. The mindset of each determines their actions, and their actions determine their outcomes.

The Danger of Protecting vs. the Power of Pushing Forward

These same dynamic plays out in leadership, sports and business. Consider the NFL. A team that takes an early lead often shifts to a defensive mindset, playing to protect their advantage rather than extend it.

Statistically, this is a dangerous approach. Teams that try to run out the clock, play conservatively and avoid risks often find themselves on the losing end. They give their opponents time to adjust, find weaknesses and regain momentum.

On the other hand, teams that stay aggressive and continue to attack even with a lead have a much higher probability of success. They dictate the game rather than react to it. The statistics support this: teams that shift to conservative play calling too early often see their win probability drop significantly in the final minutes of the game.

The Challenge of Shifting Back to Offense

One of the biggest risks of going into defensive mode too soon is the difficulty of shifting back to an offensive mindset when the situation demands it. When a team or a leader gets too comfortable with protection, their hormone levels, energy and aggressive instincts drop. The body and mind shift into a risk-averse state, which makes it difficult to suddenly regain the sharpness, confidence and execution needed to win.

In sports, when a team that has been playing it safe suddenly realizes they need to score again, they often find themselves unprepared. Their timing is off, their energy is low, and the urgency they need isn't there. The same happens in business and leadership.

When you've been defending for too long, stepping back into an offensive role takes time and effort that you may not have. The hesitation, the doubt, and the lack of momentum make regaining control far more challenging than if you had stayed aggressive in the first place.

How This Applies to Leadership

As a leader, you must recognize whether you are in a position of protection or disruption. If you have built something valuable, of course, you must defend it, but you cannot do so at the cost of stagnation. Protection without progress leads to decline. Conversely, if you are still building, you must be willing to challenge norms, push limits and take calculated risks.

The best leaders find a balance. They protect what matters while maintaining an aggressive, forward-thinking mindset. They don't let fear of loss dictate their strategy. Whether in business, sports, or life, the ones who continue to push forward and refuse to settle are the ones who ultimately shape the world around them.

So, ask yourself: Are you protecting what you have or are you fighting for what you want? The answer will determine how far you go.

Chapter 21
The Thought of Pain and
Suffering Is the Worst Part

In leadership, business and life, people often fall into the trap of trying to predict every possible outcome before acting. While preparation is valuable, an obsession with forecasting the future can lead to unnecessary stress, hesitation and even failure. The truth is that pain and suffering don't come from the unknown; they come from the fear of the unknown. Overanalyzing, overplanning, and constantly trying to predict what *might* happen can paralyze progress and create unnecessary anxiety.

The Trap of Overprediction

Predicting the future is an illusion. We can plan, strategize, and anticipate trends, but there will always be variables beyond our control. The more weight we place on trying to ensure a perfect outcome, the heavier our stress becomes. Leaders who constantly worry about *what if* instead of *what is* miss opportunities and delay decisions that could lead to growth.

This constant need for certainty creates suffering because:

- The future is unpredictable, no matter how much planning you do.

- Over-preparation creates hesitation and fear of action.

- The need for certainty removes the confidence to adapt.

The real key to success isn't predicting the future, it's *being adaptable enough to handle it when it comes.*

Solution: Have Confidence in Your Ability to Change

The most successful leaders and individuals don't fear the future because they trust their ability to adapt. The mindset shift is simple: instead of trying to control every variable, have confidence that *you* can adjust to whatever comes your way.

A simple rule to live by: *Give me two weeks' notice and I can adjust to whatever is necessary to become successful.*

This mindset allows you to:

Release the anxiety of needing all the answers ahead of time.

Act without fear of failing due to unforeseen changes.

Develop resilience instead of relying on prediction.

When you believe in your own ability to shift, pivot and adjust, you remove the weight of predicting the future and replace it with confidence in your response to it.

Solution: Learn to Take Advantage of the Present

The present is the only thing you can truly control. By focusing on the now, you put yourself in the best position for success *when* the future arrives. Leaders who maximize the present are better equipped to handle what comes next.

Know that you have the ability to adapt. You are not stagnant; you are evolving. Trust that when change happens, you will respond effectively.

Understand that you can't control external influences. No matter how much you plan, there will always be external factors such as economic shifts, competitors or unexpected disruptions.

Instead of trying to predict them all, focus on being flexible enough to handle them when they arrive.

Make decisions with the information you have today. Overweighting future prediction leads to inaction. Take the best step forward now, knowing you can adjust as needed.

Embracing Adaptability Over Fear

The most resilient leaders are not the ones who perfectly predict the future; they are the ones who trust their ability to adjust when the future arrives.

Don't suffer over what you can't control.

Don't let fear of the unknown keep you from acting.

Trust that when change comes, you will be ready.

The weight of predicting the future is too heavy to carry. The freedom of adaptability is what leads to true success.

Chapter 22
The Tyranny of Distance

The Tyranny of Distance in Business Relationships

In military strategy, the term tyranny of distance refers to the challenge of projecting power and sustaining operations over vast geographical separations.

The U.S. Air Force has long grappled with this issue, particularly in the Indo-Pacific region, where aircraft and personnel must operate effectively despite logistical challenges posed by great distances.

Overcoming these obstacles requires innovative solutions such as extended aircraft range, aerial refueling and strategic deployment of resources to maintain operational superiority.

The same principle applies to business. When working with clients across different geographies, distance creates an inherent challenge to building strong relationships. Just as the military must extend its reach through strategic innovations, businesses must proactively create intimacy and engagement despite geographical separation.

The further away a client is, the more intentional we must be in fostering connection, building trust and demonstrating value.

Bridging the Distance: Creating Intimacy in Client Relationships

Effective business relationships thrive on trust, communication and perceived value. When working with clients in different locations, leaders must be deliberate in finding ways to bridge the distance. Physical separation can easily lead to disengagement, reduced loyalty and a transactional relationship if not managed effectively.

Video Meetings: Replacing Proximity with Presence

> While nothing can fully replace face-to-face interactions, video meetings create a stronger connection than emails or phone calls alone. A client who regularly sees your face, observes your expressions, and hears the tone of your voice will feel a deeper sense of engagement. Tools like Zoom, Microsoft Teams, or Google Meet help replicate the feeling of being in the same room, reducing the emotional gap created by distance.

Unique Communication Techniques: More Than Just Emails

> Over-reliance on email can make a client relationship feel distant and impersonal. Mixing in voice messages, short video clips or even personalized handwritten notes can create a sense of exclusivity and thoughtfulness. Leaders who leverage diverse communication methods stand out and make their clients feel valued.

Software Solutions: Enhancing Accessibility and Engagement

> Just as the military invests in technological solutions to overcome distance in combat, businesses must leverage technology to enhance client relationships. Client portals, interactive dashboards and collaborative project management tools help maintain transparency and streamline communication. CRM (Customer Relationship Management) systems, such as Salesforce or HubSpot,

allow businesses to track interactions, preferences and engagement levels to ensure a personalized approach to client needs.

Strategic On-Site Visits: Quality Over Quantity

While frequent travel to every client may not be feasible, strategically planned visits to key clients can create meaningful touchpoints. A well-timed, purposeful in-person visit strengthens trust and reinforces commitment to the relationship. When combined with consistent virtual engagement, these visits have even greater impact.

Understanding the Levels of Communication

Communication intimacy in business relationships varies based on the method chosen. Recognizing these levels helps leaders select the most effective method to strengthen relationships:

Live Face-to-Face: The most intimate, allowing direct emotional exchange and immediate feedback, fostering deep trust. This is where tough conversations must live.

Video Face-to-Face: High intimacy through visual engagement, allowing for emotional cues and enhanced connection. New information and conversations requiring feedback fit well here. Also, when time is of the essence and a live face to face would take too long to initiate.

Phone: Moderate intimacy, providing emotional nuance through voice tone without visual cues. In today's world, this should be a rare need, but travel and inability to access video can make this a necessity over lower levels of intimacy. Too many people dive into email to hide from engaging someone in real time. follow-up:

Don't fall into that trap as it will turn into painful outcomes more often than you would expect.

Text: Lower intimacy, suitable for quick updates but lacking depth and emotional context. Great for follow-up and quick updates that need immediate attention.

Email: Low intimacy, effective for formal communication, but risks impersonality if overused. Great as a form of recapping or verifying details of prior conversations. Try to never use it for new information or any difficult conversations.

Regular Mail: Unique intimacy through personal effort and tangibility, conveying thoughtfulness and personal attention.

Communication Through Others: Least intimate, useful for conveying information indirectly, but can dilute personal connection and can cause misunderstandings.

Communication Intimacy with Employees

Similar to client relationships, the level of intimacy in employee communications has a significant impact on organizational culture and effectiveness.

Employees who regularly engage in face-to-face interactions, whether live or via video, tend to experience greater job satisfaction, trust and commitment to organizational goals.

Phone calls offer personal connection and emotional nuance, valuable for performance discussions or sensitive matters. Text and email, while efficient, should be balanced carefully, as over-reliance can lead to feelings of impersonality and isolation.

Thoughtful use of regular mail, such as personalized notes or recognition letters, adds a unique depth of connection, making employees feel genuinely valued. Finally, relying too heavily on communication through others can dilute managerial influence, weaken leadership presence and diminish employee engagement.

The Right Level of Communication Intimacy

A military force must find the right balance between overextending itself and being too distant to be effective, similarly, businesses must calibrate their client and employee engagement levels. Too little communication can create disconnection, while too much can overwhelm or feel intrusive. The key is to assess each client's and employee's preferences and expectations, tailoring the level of communication intimacy accordingly.

Winning the Battle Against Distance

Just as the Air Force extends its operational reach through innovation and strategic deployment, business leaders must develop creative solutions to overcome the tyranny of distance in client and employee relationships. By leveraging technology, diversifying communication methods and strategically planning interactions, businesses can cultivate strong, lasting relationships regardless of geographical barriers.

The organizations that master this balance don't just maintain their client base, they deepen trust, increase engagement and set themselves apart as irreplaceable partners in success.

Chapter 23
Don't Undervalue the Impact of Your Leadership Voice

One of the most underestimated aspects of leadership is the power of communication. Every word a leader speaks carries weight, often more than they realize. In the world of social media, typing in *ALL CAPS* is interpreted as yelling. It grabs attention, conveys intensity, and can sometimes overwhelm the reader. The same concept applies to leadership. When a leader speaks, it is received as if it were in *ALL CAPS*, loud, impactful, and often deeply personal to those hearing it.

The Weight of a Leader's Words

As a leader, you are always being listened to and watched. Whether addressing a room full of employees, giving one-on-one feedback or even making an offhand comment in a casual setting, your words are amplified in the minds of those you lead. This applies to both praise and criticism:

- A simple *"great job"* can feel like a career-defining moment.

- A passing *"this could have been better"* can feel like a major failure.

- A leader's frustration can ripple through an organization like an earthquake.

- A leader's enthusiasm can fuel motivation and commitment at unprecedented levels.

What you say, and how you say it, shapes the morale, confidence and performance of your team.

The Intentionality of Leadership Communication

Because everything a leader says is heard *louder* than intended, great leaders develop an awareness of their communication. They don't leave their words to chance. They are intentional in how they deliver messages, understanding that their voice sets the tone for the entire organization.

Be Clear and Purposeful

Avoid ambiguity in your words. Employees will read between the lines, even when there's nothing there. If you express doubt, they will sense instability. If you express excitement, they will rally around your energy. Be clear about your expectations, vision and feedback.

Control Your Emotions When Speaking

If a leader speaks out of frustration, even momentarily, it can be perceived as a sweeping criticism of an individual or team. While passion is important, being mindful of your tone and emotional state ensures that your words encourage rather than deflate. Leaders who constantly react emotionally create a tense environment where employees feel they must walk on eggshells.

Balance Praise and Constructive Feedback

Because everything you say is amplified, finding the right balance between positive reinforcement and correction is crucial. Over-praising can dilute the impact of recognition, while excessive critique can demoralize. Leaders must ensure that their communication builds confidence while also guiding improvement.

Understanding the Psychological Impact of Leadership Communication

Psychologically, people are wired to give more weight to negative comments than positive ones. Studies show that it takes multiple positive interactions to counteract one negative experience. Leaders must keep this in mind when providing feedback or addressing their teams.

- If you give feedback in a group setting, be aware that employees will compare how you addressed them versus their peers.

- If you recognize one employee's success, others may internalize a perceived lack of recognition.

- If you express doubt in a decision, your team may assume a crisis is ahead.

Speak with Awareness

Great leaders understand that their words are magnified. They embrace the responsibility of communication, knowing that their voice carries influence beyond their immediate intention. Whether delivering praise, direction, or constructive criticism, they ensure their words are intentional, clear and aligned with their leadership vision.

Every word you say as a leader is heard in *ALL CAPS*. Make sure it's worth hearing.

Chapter 24
The Laws They Forgot To
Teach In Law School

Part 1 – The Law of Unintended Consequences

We are taught many laws in life, but one law doesn't seem to be taught or even understood by many in life and business. That law is the Law of Unintended Consequences.

Every decision a leader makes sets off a chain reaction. While the intended outcome may be clear, the ripple effects, both positive and negative, can be unpredictable. This phenomenon is known as *The Law of Unintended Consequences*. Great leaders recognize that decision-making isn't just about solving a problem in the moment; it's about anticipating the broader impact of their choices.

Types of Unintended Consequences

1. **Unexpected Benefits** – Sometimes, a decision produces positive side effects beyond what was anticipated. For example, a company implementing a flexible remote work policy to attract talent may find that it also increases productivity and reduces operational costs.

2. **Unexpected Drawbacks** – Many decisions create new challenges. A business may automate customer service to cut costs, only to find that customer satisfaction drops due to a lack of human interaction.

3. **Perverse Outcomes** – The worst type of unintended consequence occurs when a decision backfires entirely,

creating the opposite of the intended effect. For example, banning overtime to reduce employee burnout may instead lead to increased stress as employees rush to complete work within standard hours.

The Ripple Effect of Decisions

Decision makers who fail to look beyond the immediate effect often create larger problems than they initially set out to solve. Conversely, those who take the time to think critically about *all* potential consequences, intended or not, position themselves and their teams for long-term success.

The Leadership Skill of Seeing Beyond the Obvious

Great leaders train themselves to think beyond the first layer of impact. They consider:

- Who will be affected beyond the immediate stakeholders?

- What behaviors will this decision encourage or discourage?

- What could go wrong that I haven't considered?

- What adjustments can be made now to prevent unintended consequences later?

Real-World Example: The Soda Tax

In an effort to combat obesity, several cities introduced a tax on sugary drinks, expecting that higher prices would reduce consumption. While the tax did lower soda sales, it also led to unintended economic consequences.

Many consumers traveled to neighboring cities to buy their drinks tax-free, harming local businesses without significantly improving public health. The initial goal was noble, but the unintended effects had to be reevaluated.

How to Avoid Unintended Consequences

1. **Think in Systems, Not Silos** – Every decision will impact multiple areas. Step back and assess the broader ecosystem before implementing a major change.

2. **Pressure Test Decisions** – Seek diverse perspectives before deciding. A well-rounded discussion often reveals hidden risks.

3. **Pilot Before Full Execution** – Testing decisions on a small scale first can expose unintended consequences before they become major problems.

4. **Stay Adaptable** – Even the best leaders won't anticipate everything. The key is recognizing unintended consequences quickly and adjusting accordingly.

Intentional Leadership

The Law of Unintended Consequences is not about avoiding decisions; it's about making better ones. Leaders who take the time to analyze the potential ripple effects of their choices create sustainable success. They recognize that every move they make has a broader impact and take responsibility for seeing beyond the immediate outcome.

Making decisions is easy. Making *great* decisions requires wisdom, foresight and the willingness to anticipate the unexpected.

Chapter 25
The Laws They Forgot To
Teach In Law School

Part 2 – The Law of Supply and Demand

If you ever sat through a law school class, you undoubtedly learned about torts, contracts, property, and maybe even tax law, but you likely didn't learn the most powerful law affecting your everyday life: The Law of Supply and Demand. It's a straightforward principle, yet astonishingly overlooked, considering it governs nearly every decision we make.

Supply-and-demand isn't merely an economic theory buried in dusty textbooks. It's the unseen force behind everything, from finding your soulmate to scoring tickets to the biggest concert in town. When you grasp this profound yet straightforward law, your life, leadership, and decision-making can become infinitely easier and far more rewarding.

The Basics, Simplified

At its core, the law of supply and demand says that if something is abundant (high supply) and few people want it (low demand), it becomes inexpensive or undervalued. Conversely, if something is rare (low supply) and highly desired (high demand), it becomes expensive or highly valued.

Now let's translate this economic jargon into real life.

Finding Love Through Economics

Take dating as a prime example. Ever wonder why "playing hard to get" is such timeless advice? Because scarcity creates value. If you're always available (high supply), your desirability decreases. But if your availability is limited (low supply), suddenly demand skyrockets. You become intriguing. People want what feels exclusive.

Remember, though, don't overdo it with scarcity, or you'll become inaccessible. Balance the scales: enough scarcity to increase value, enough availability to maintain interest.

The Concert Ticket Conundrum

If your favorite band announces a limited run of reunion concerts, only ten shows worldwide, demand immediately surges through the roof and suddenly tickets are priced like rare gemstones. The fans willing and able to pay the most secure their seats.

Understand this, and you won't grumble about ticket prices; you'll realize you're witnessing economics at work. You either pay the premium (high demand, low supply) or accept enjoying.

Getting the Job You Want

Job markets operate on the same principle. Specialized, hard-to-acquire skills (low supply) command higher salaries and job security because many companies want them (high demand). Think software engineers who understand artificial intelligence, these roles pay handsomely because the demand outweighs supply.

If you're feeling undervalued in your career, maybe it's time to increase your rarity. Acquire new skills, certifications or specializations that put you in low supply but high demand.

Their playlist from home.

Applying the Law in Leadership

Smart leaders intuitively understand supply and demand. They know their time and expertise are valuable precisely because they're limited resources. Leaders who make themselves overly accessible diminish their perceived value and effectiveness. Conversely, a leader who carefully manages their availability, reserving it for high-impact moments, can amplify their influence and effectiveness.

Keeping it Light: Supply and Demand in Everyday Life

Even everyday decisions, like choosing what to do with your weekend or picking a restaurant, hinge on supply and demand. A trendy eatery with limited seating commands reservations weeks in advance. Yet, a place open 24/7 rarely sees a packed house.

The beauty of the law of supply and demand is its simplicity and power to clarify. Once you understand it, you'll navigate life with less frustration and more strategic success.

Remember: everything in life is a balance of how much there is versus how much it's wanted. Master this principle, and you'll enjoy less friction and greater fulfillment in relationships, careers, leisure and leadership. It might just be the best "law" you never learned in law school.

Chapter 26
Building Success With and Through Others

By not wanting success for others, you energetically block your own success.

Success is not a finite resource. Yet, many people operate as if another person's success diminishes their own. This scarcity mindset creates invisible barriers, not just for those they resent, but for themselves. The energy of competition, jealousy, or unwillingness to support others can become a self-imposed obstacle, blocking opportunities, creativity, and personal growth.

The Energy of Abundance vs. Scarcity

People who actively celebrate and encourage the success of others tend to find more success themselves. This isn't just a feel-good philosophy; it's a principle that has been proven in business, sports, and leadership. When you shift your mindset to genuinely supporting others, you open yourself to new connections, fresh ideas and a network of people who will, in turn, support you.

On the flip side, when you resist the success of others, you unconsciously put up walls. Your energy becomes defensive rather than creative, and rather than focusing on growth, you focus on why others don't deserve what they have. This negative focus drains mental energy that could be used for innovation, leadership, and progress.

Sacrificial Leadership: The Key to Unlocking Success

Zig Ziglar famously said, *"You can have everything in life you want if you will just help enough other people get what they want."*

This is the essence of sacrificial leadership—leading not for personal gain, but with the intent to uplift others. True leaders understand that by investing in the success of those around them, they create a cycle of abundance that ultimately benefits everyone, including themselves.

When you embrace sacrificial leadership, you stop seeing success as a competition and start viewing it as a collective journey. Helping others achieve their goals does not delay or diminish your success; it accelerates it. Leaders who practice this principle build stronger teams, cultivate loyalty, and create environments where innovation and collaboration thrive.

Maslow's Hierarchy of Needs: Moving Toward Greater Purpose

Understanding why some people struggle to support others' success can often be traced back to Maslow's hierarchy of needs. Maslow's theory proposes human needs are arranged in a hierarchical pyramid (Physiological/Survival, Safety, Love and Belonging, Esteem, and finally Self-Actualization). The basic needs start with survival, and the highest needs are purpose-based. If you are constantly focused on survival, worrying about financial stability, basic security or personal recognition, it becomes difficult to operate with an abundance mindset. When you are stuck at the lower levels of the hierarchy (physiological and safety needs), your energy is consumed by self-preservation rather than a greater purpose.

However, as you progress through Maslow's pyramid, moving from basic needs to love and belonging, esteem, and ultimately self-actualization, you develop the ability to think beyond yourself. Leaders who operate at the highest level of the hierarchy focus on impact, legacy and service. They understand that true fulfillment doesn't come from hoarding success but from sharing it.

If you find yourself resistant to supporting others, ask: *Am I too focused on survival? Am I neglecting my opportunity to contribute to something greater?* Recognizing where you are in this framework can help you shift your mindset toward abundance and long-term success.

Life Stories of the Blocking Mindset

The Resentful Employee Who Stalled His Own Career

John had been with his company for over ten years. He worked hard but felt overlooked when younger employees were promoted ahead of him. Instead of learning from their success and adapting his approach, he stewed in resentment. He downplayed their achievements, criticized their methods and refused to collaborate. Over time, his negativity became evident to leadership. He wasn't seen as a team player or a leader. As a result, promotions continued to pass him by, not because he wasn't talented but because his mindset blocked his own growth.

The Business Owner Who Fostered a Culture of Growth

Susan, a small business owner, understood the power of lifting others up. When one of her employees, Mark, expressed a desire to start his own company, rather than seeing him as a threat, she mentored him. She introduced him to contacts, gave him business advice, and even sent clients his way. Years later, Mark's company flourished, and he, in turn, sent major opportunities back to Susan. Her willingness to encourage success beyond her own walls ended up expanding her own business in ways she never expected.

How to Remove the Blocks to Your Own Success

1. **Celebrate the Success of Others** – Actively acknowledge and support the achievements of colleagues, competitors, and peers. When you see someone succeed, instead of feeling envious, ask yourself, *What can I learn from them?*

2. **Adopt a Growth Mindset** – Success is not a zero-sum game. Someone else winning does not mean you are losing. Believe that opportunities are abundant and that your own path will unfold in due time.

3. **Give Without Expecting Immediate Returns** – Offer support, share knowledge, and help others without looking for direct benefits. Often, the rewards come later in unexpected ways.

4. **Focus on Your Own Path** – Instead of comparing yourself to others, channel your energy into improving your skills, expanding your network, and taking action toward your own goals.

5. **Create a Success-Oriented Environment** – Surround yourself with people who uplift and inspire. Toxic environments foster competition and resentment, while positive environments create growth for everyone.

The Freedom in Supporting Others

When you genuinely want success for others, you free yourself from the mental and emotional weight of comparison and resentment. This shift allows you to focus on your own journey, create meaningful relationships, and attract opportunities that might otherwise have been blocked.

Success is not about taking from others, it's about growing together. The sooner you embrace this; the sooner you'll remove the barriers standing in your own way.

Chapter 27
Protection Is The Key

Since You Can't Protect Yourself from Everything, Start by Protecting Everything from Yourself

Many people go through life obsessed with avoiding risks, eliminating uncertainty and protecting themselves from anything that *could* go wrong. They plan endlessly, worry about worst-case scenarios, and make decisions rooted in fear rather than logic. But what if the real problem isn't the external threats we try so hard to guard against? What if the real threat is *ourselves*, our own flawed decision-making, biases and unnecessary worries?

Self-Induced Misery: The Biggest Threat We Face

Most of the mistakes and suffering we experience in life are not caused by external forces but by *self-inflicted* poor decisions. Bad predictions, bad judgment, and the cost of doing nothing are the primary drivers of regret. Many of us make decisions based on imagined fears rather than rational analysis.

Consider this: *Sometimes, doing nothing is the smartest move.* The constant urge to react, to do something just for the sake of taking action, often leads to unnecessary stress and bad outcomes. Worrying about everything, from hurricanes to economic downturns to political shifts, doesn't change the outcome. It only wastes energy and creates unnecessary anxiety.

The Business Owners Who Sold Too Soon

A perfect example of self-inflicted loss happened in 2020 when many business owners sold their companies out of fear. The concern? A U.S. presidential change would raise capital gains tax rates from 23.5% to ordinary income tax levels.

The reality? That tax law never changed during the next four years. Meanwhile, the economy and financial markets saw strong growth. Many of these business owners missed out on higher valuations and greater profit distributions. One company that sold at 11x earnings (profit) saw its industry experience a 40% growth over the next four years, with profit multiples expanding to 14x. Had they held onto the business, their decision could have been worth *tens of millions of dollars more.*

Their attempt to *protect* themselves from a perceived risk ended up costing them far more than the risk itself.

Fear of Loss: The Bias That Holds You Back

Daniel Kahneman, a Nobel Prize winning behavioral scientist, discovered a fundamental truth about human decision-making: *People act on the fear of loss at a 2:1 ratio over the potential for gain.*

This means that the desire to avoid loss is twice as powerful as the motivation to pursue success. And this fear-based mindset can lead to a life of hesitation, missed opportunities and ultimately, regret.

When you're constantly trying to shield yourself from every possible negative outcome, you inadvertently block yourself from growth, success and new opportunities. The key isn't to eliminate all risks, it's to recognize that the biggest risks often come from overprotecting yourself.

Happiness vs. Avoiding Suffering

Many people struggle with defining *happiness*, but almost everyone can clearly define *unhappiness*: Suffering.

Ironically, the harder we try to avoid discomfort, the more suffering we often create for ourselves. The person who never takes a chance on a new career path, never starts a business or never invests in their own potential often ends up in the most painful situation of all, *regret.*

The Ferrari vs. The Old Truck

Imagine you buy an old, beat-up truck. You can park it anywhere; drive it anywhere and never worry about scratches or dings. It gives you freedom.

Now imagine you buy a Ferrari. Suddenly, every parking spot is a risk. You park miles away to avoid door dings, worry constantly about scratches and stress over every bump in the road. The very thing that was supposed to bring happiness, the Ferrari, now causes *more* anxiety and unhappiness than the old truck ever did.

This is a perfect metaphor for life: *The more we try to protect ourselves from everything, the more we end up trapping ourselves in stress and fear.*

Be the Master of Your Own Risk

The real key to success isn't in eliminating risks, it's in recognizing the difference between rational preparation and fear-driven decision making.

- Are you making choices based on facts or based on imagined fears?

- Are you avoiding suffering or creating more of it through unnecessary stress?

- Are you overprotecting yourself and missing out on the true rewards of life?

Instead of focusing on protecting yourself from everything, start by making sure you're not the one standing in your own way. The moment you let go of unnecessary fear, you free yourself to make better decisions, embrace opportunity and live with fewer regrets.

Chapter 28
Fish Don't Eat Hooks, They Eat Bait

Ask any fisherman, fish don't bite hooks, they bite bait. The hook is necessary, but the bait makes it attractive. Leadership isn't much different. Great leaders understand that the tasks and challenges they present must come with appealing motivations, bait, to effectively engage their team.

Hook and Bait

Imagine you're a manager tasked with improving customer service scores. Telling your team, "We need higher scores" is like dangling an empty hook, it's unappealing, perhaps even painful. But what if you attached enticing bait, such as meaningful recognition or a clear vision of career advancement opportunities? Now you have their attention. The same tough objective suddenly seems appealing, achievable, even exciting.

The Magic of the Gold Star

When Matthew first took over a struggling sales department, morale was low, and numbers were worse. He introduced the simplest form of bait imaginable: gold star stickers. At first, salespeople laughed, thinking stickers were silly. But soon, each gold star posted beside someone's name on a public board became a visible badge of pride. Friendly competition erupted, camaraderie grew, and before long, the stickers translated into improved morale, boosted sales and eventually bonuses. Matthew understood human nature, we might not eat hooks, but we'll chase enticing bait, even if it's as simple as recognition.

Framing the Picture

Anna, a seasoned executive, faced the difficult task of cutting costs at her company. Layoffs loomed and anxiety was high. Instead of presenting it solely as a painful process (the hook), she reframed the effort with powerful bait: the promise of saving jobs by rallying together. She transparently explained how shared sacrifice, innovation and teamwork could avoid layoffs entirely. This inspired her team to embrace cost-cutting creatively. Employees willingly trimmed unnecessary expenses, generated innovative ideas, and built solidarity. Ultimately, the team avoided layoffs entirely, emerging more cohesive and motivated than ever.

Keeping Spirits High When Waters Get Rough

Leadership also means helping your team persist through tough times. Just as bait encourages fish to bite even in less-than-ideal conditions, encouragement keeps a team moving forward when the waters are choppy.

Samuel led a small startup facing repeated product failures. Frustration and burnout were setting in. Samuel knew raw determination wouldn't suffice, so he introduced "Fail Forward Fridays." Each Friday, employees shared lessons learned from the week's mistakes, with the best insight earning a coveted "Trophy of Bravery", a humorous, oversized rubber duck. This tradition turned setbacks into celebrations of progress, transforming frustration into laughter, resilience and creativity. Samuel didn't remove the hook, business is tough, but he provided bait so appealing that the challenges became opportunities to thrive.

The Leadership Takeaway

Fish don't bite because they're eager to encounter metal hooks; they bite because the bait is irresistible. As leaders, our job isn't to disguise difficulty but to create genuine, appealing incentives, recognition, growth opportunities and shared purpose, that motivate others to overcome challenges.

So, consider this: What's your bait? What genuine incentives and heartfelt encouragement will you offer to motivate your team through their toughest tasks? Remember, fish don't eat hooks, they eat bait.

Chapter 29
Conquerors Foster Rebellion

Throughout history, in leadership, parenting, and business, a fundamental truth emerges: those who are conquered will eventually rebel. When power is exerted purely through dominance, fear or control without belief and conviction, it creates a slow-building resistance that ultimately leads to rebellion. True leadership is not about forcing compliance; it's about inspiring commitment.

Power vs. Conviction: The Failure of 'Because I Said So'

One of the greatest mistakes leaders, parents and business executives make is believing that positional power is enough. *"Because I said so"* may work in the short term, but it does not create lasting loyalty or commitment. When people feel forced into compliance without understanding or agreeing with the decision, they will eventually find ways to resist, whether subtly or outright.

History has proven that ruling by force often leads to rebellion. Monarchies have fallen, dictatorships have been overthrown, and even corporate executives have lost their grip when employees or consumers push back against control without conviction. The greatest leaders don't rely on mandates alone, they create belief.

The Limits of Money, Position, and Size

Power that relies solely on financial strength, hierarchical position or sheer size is temporary. While it may win in the moment, it often creates deep resentment among those on the losing end. The underdog, often smaller, financially weaker or lower in position, can outmaneuver and outlast a dominant force if they have intelligence, strategy and conviction on their side.

Consider the story of David and Goliath. The giant had strength and size, but David had precision, intelligence and purpose. In business, we see this play out when industry giants fail to adapt, and smaller, more innovative companies disrupt the market. Kodak, Blockbuster and countless others have learned this lesson too late.

The Power of Example Over Domination

The most influential leaders lead by example. Rather than demanding compliance, they inspire action by embodying the values and behaviors they wish to see in others. Influence is far more powerful than authority, and people are more likely to follow those they respect and admire than those they fear.

A great leader doesn't need to demand loyalty, it is earned. Employees work harder for a boss they respect. Children are more likely to adopt values they see lived out rather than just being told what to do. In every domain, leadership through example creates genuine buy-in rather than forced obedience.

The Art of Making It Their Idea

One of the most powerful skills in leadership is the ability to guide someone to a decision *without making them feel forced into it.* When people believe something is their own idea, their commitment to it skyrockets. This requires patience, guidance and the ability to present perspectives in a way that allows others to reach the conclusion themselves.

When someone makes a decision with conviction rather than coercion, they take ownership of it. This is where real change and lasting commitment are born.

Parenting Example: The Short Shorts Rebellion

A mother faced a dilemma with her daughter, who wanted to wear short shorts to the last day of high school, despite it being against the school dress code. Many students planned to break the rule since there would be no real consequences on the last day.

Rather than use the usual *"because I said so"* to forbid her daughter to wear the short shorts, one mother took a different approach, she had an open conversation. She explained that while short shorts were acceptable in some settings, deliberately breaking a rule for convenience was not a reflection of strong character. She emphasized that the choice was about her daughter's personal brand and the kind of person she wanted to be.

After a thoughtful discussion, the daughter decided on her own not to wear the shorts. Though this was what was expected, the mother wanted to reward the daughter for her good judgment in hopes of replicating in the future. So, that afternoon, her mother rewarded her with a pair of sneakers she had been wanting. When they went shopping, the daughter shared how her best friend had a major argument with her mother, who had declared, *"You will not wear those shorts because I said so!"* The girl, feeling conquered, snuck the shorts in her bag and changed at school. Her act of rebellion stemmed from being overpowered rather than guided.

Business Lesson: Influence vs. Forced Compliance

In business, power is not about forcing people to comply but about inspiring them to act willingly. The most successful organizations foster cultures where employees and customers *want* to engage, not where they feel they *have* to comply.

- A leader who dictates without explanation will struggle with disengagement and turnover.

- A company that forces rigid policies without input will face resistance and inefficiency.

- A brand that tries to manipulate consumers rather than build trust will eventually lose market share to companies that create genuine loyalty.

The greatest power comes from earned influence, the kind that develops when people choose to follow, contribute and engage because they believe in the mission, the leadership, and the values being lived out.

Inspire, Don't Conquer

Those who are conquered will eventually rebel. If your only tool is dominance, your influence is temporary. If your power is based on trust, example and guiding people to their own convictions, your impact will be lasting.

Chapter 30
Who Took Away My Curriculum, Scoreboard and Appetite?

The Shift from Structure to Self-Direction

For most of our early lives, we move through structured environments, school, college, and training programs, all of which provide a clear roadmap. There is a defined curriculum, a structured syllabus and predetermined expectations. We know what we need to do: attend classes, complete assignments, and follow the outlined process.

Then, one day, we step into the real world. The roadmap disappears. There are no more teachers telling us what to study next, no more syllabi outlining how to progress and no built-in scoreboard to measure if we are winning or losing.

At this moment, many people freeze. They wait for someone to hand them the next curriculum and the next set of instructions. But here's the truth, if you are waiting for someone to build your curriculum for life, you'll wait forever. The responsibility to define your own path is now yours.

Building Your Own Curriculum

In the professional world, if you want to achieve something, whether it's starting a business, excelling in a career or mastering a skill, you must construct your own learning process. The difference between those who succeed and those who drift aimlessly is the ability to map out their own curriculum.

- *What do I need to learn?*

- *Who can I learn from?*

- *What experiences will accelerate my growth?*

- *How will I measure progress?*

The moment you take ownership of your own development, you stop being a passive participant and become the architect of your future.

Creating Your Own Scoreboard

In school, we have a clear scoreboard: grades, test scores and class rankings. In sports, there's a visible scoreboard and a clock counting down the game. Without these, the competition turns into aimless activity, players just running around, catching balls and tackling each other without a sense of purpose.

In the workplace, the scoreboard is often missing or unclear. If the company doesn't provide a structured way to track progress, you must create your own. Otherwise, you risk just showing up every day, staying busy and wondering if you are making any real progress.

A well-defined scoreboard includes:

- **Short-term indicators** – Success in your current job (projects completed, client satisfaction, skill development).

- **Long-term indicators** – Career progression, personal development, life fulfillment.

- **Purpose-driven tracking** – Measuring impact beyond just money (leadership, influence, contribution).

If your only measure of success is money, you will never have enough, and you will lack qualitative markers of fulfillment. A career without a well-rounded scoreboard is like a game with no defined outcome, it's just movement without meaning.

Bringing More Than an Appetite to the Table

In school, you show up like a guest at Thanksgiving dinner. The meal is prepared, the table is set and all you have to do is eat. In college, the structure remains, you are served the lessons, the materials and the schedule. But in life and business, just showing up with an appetite is not enough.

If you want to truly succeed, you must:

1. **Plan the Meal** – Know what you want to accomplish, what ingredients (skills and experiences) you need, and what the final outcome should look like.

2. **Cook the Food** – Do the hard work, learn the processes and develop the ability to execute.

3. **Serve Others** – Success isn't just about what you consume but what you contribute.

4. **Clean Up** – Reflect, adjust and prepare for the next opportunity.

If you only show up to consume, whether in business or in life, you'll never fully understand how things work, nor will you develop the depth of skills necessary for long-term success.

The Missing Pieces

Nobody tells you when you leave a structured environment that from this point forward, you must build your own curriculum, create your own scoreboard, and bring more than just an appetite to the table. These three things determine who thrives and who simply drifts:

- Without a curriculum, you wait for direction instead of forging your own path.

- Without a scoreboard, you wander without knowing if you're winning or losing.

- Without an active appetite, you consume but never contribute, learn but never apply.

The most successful people in any field are those who recognize that school was just preparation. The real game begins when you take control of your own education, define your own success metrics, and fully engage in the process, not just as a consumer, but as a creator.

Are you waiting for someone to hand you the playbook, or are you ready to write your own?

Chapter 31
The Calculus of Wisdom

What Creates the Illusion of Wisdom?

Everyone starts life knowing nothing. Yet, as we grow, we seek to gain knowledge, share insights and ultimately be considered wise. But wisdom is not simply about acquiring information; it is about how and when we share it. The process of becoming wise can be thought of as an equation:

Wisdom = (Advice Given) × (Accuracy of Advice)

- If you give **no advice**, you remain invisible. You are not in the game.

- If you give **a lot of advice** but it is consistently wrong, you are considered a fool.

- If you give **accurate advice**, people start to see you as wise.

At some point, you must take the risk of offering advice. The key is recognizing when it is time to refine that advice, work toward accuracy and earn the right to be trusted.

The Ultimate Reward: Being Considered Wise

One of the greatest rewards in life is being sought out for wisdom. People will only take advice from those they perceive as wise. The opposite of wisdom is foolishness, and no one seeks guidance from a fool. If you aspire to influence, lead or mentor, you must first earn credibility.

How do you achieve this? You must demonstrate competence, genuine care and the ability to truly understand the needs of others. When people trust that you are offering advice in their best interest, they will listen. If they sense that you are uninformed, self-serving or disconnected, they will tune you out.

The Pain of Bad Advice

People don't just hear advice, they feel it. If someone follows your guidance and gets hurt, they experience pain at two levels: the actual consequences of the advice and the emotional disappointment of misplaced trust.

If your advice leads to negative outcomes, the individual will hesitate to seek your counsel again. The moment people associate your guidance with failure or harm, they will stop listening. This is why wisdom is not just about having answers, it's about knowing when to give advice, when to hold back and when to refine your understanding before speaking.

Wisdom as an Art, Not an Obligation

Great advisors are not emotionally attached to their advice. They understand that wisdom is an evolving art, not a rigid set of rules. The most effective advisors detach themselves from their own opinions, allowing room for adaptation and deeper insight.

The wisest individuals remain open to new information, willing to adjust their perspective when necessary. Those who cling to their own advice with an unyielding grip risk being seen as arrogant rather than wise.

The "Batmobile" Effect: Why Advice is Rejected

Advice is only considered when ignorance is first admitted. If someone believes they already have the answers, they will automatically reject external input.

Think of Batman's Batmobile. The moment a threat is detected, armor shields the vehicle, making it impenetrable. People do the same thing when they hear unsolicited advice. If they feel judged, misunderstood or patronized, they will *Batmobile* themselves, mentally shutting down and blocking out everything being said.

Earning the right to give advice requires first demonstrating that you genuinely care. If someone doesn't believe you have their best interests at heart, they will reject even the best advice. Wisdom is about timing, trust and connection, not just knowledge.

The Balance of Earning the Right vs. Pushing Advice

There is a delicate balance between earning the right to give advice and forcefully trying to guide someone. The key to this balance is *active listening*, not just hearing words but demonstrating a deep understanding of the other person's emotions and needs.

People don't just want to be heard; they want to be understood. When someone feels truly understood, they will ask for guidance. When they don't, they will resist it.

Consider the common relationship dynamic between a husband and wife:

- A wife tells her husband about a frustrating situation at work.

- The husband immediately begins offering solutions.

- She gets frustrated and says, *"You're not listening to me."*

- The husband defensively replies, *"I heard everything you said. I'm just trying to help you solve the problem."*

The problem isn't that he wasn't listening, it's that he didn't make her feel understood.

Now, let's replay the conversation with a subtle but powerful shift:

- The wife shares her work frustration.

- Instead of immediately offering solutions, the husband acknowledges her emotions: *"That sounds really frustrating. I can see why that upset you."*

- He shows empathy and validates her feelings.

- The wife, now feeling understood, says, *"What do you think I should do?"*

The advice is now welcomed, rather than rejected. Wisdom is not just about having the right answers, it's about understanding when and how to deliver them.

The Path to True Wisdom

The journey to wisdom is not about knowing everything, it's about mastering the art of when to speak, when to listen and when to refine your perspective. True wisdom is earned through:

1. Providing advice with accuracy, not just frequency.

2. Understanding that bad advice carries consequences.

3. Detaching from your own opinions and remaining adaptable.

4. Earning trust before offering guidance.

5. Listening actively to make others feel understood.

The wisest people in the world aren't those who talk the most, they are those who have learned when to listen, *when* to talk, *what* to say and *how* to say it. Wisdom is not a gift, it is a skill, one that requires intention, patience and practice.

Chapter 32
Watermelon Seed Management

The Harder You Squeeze, The Harder They Are to Manage

Managing people is much like handling a watermelon seed. If you've ever tried to pinch one between your fingers, you know what happens, the harder you squeeze, the further it shoots away. People are no different. The more pressure and force you exert, the more they resist, evade or even escape from your influence altogether.

Leaders and managers often unknowingly create resistance by applying the wrong type of pressure. Effective leadership isn't about force, it's about guidance. There are three primary ways to manage a watermelon seed, and these methods mirror different management styles.

Three Ways to Manage a Watermelon Seed

1. The Pinch – Maximum Pressure, Maximum Rebellion

Pinching a watermelon seed applies force from two sides, causing it to launch far away from you. In management, this represents leaders who exert excessive pressure, micromanage or place overwhelming expectations on their team. Instead of gaining control, they lose influence. Employees subjected to this kind of leadership often:

- Seek other opportunities and leave.

- Quietly disengage or resist.

- Become unresponsive, unpredictable or defensive.

114

When leaders use the pinch method, they mistakenly believe that tighter control leads to better performance. However, tighter control leads to distance and loss of trust.

2. The Ice Pick – Sharp, Isolated, and Potentially Harmful

Using an ice pick on a watermelon seed is effective in one specific area, but it destroys the seed in the process. This represents leaders who use sharp, demanding, and often unreasonable expectations. An icepick approach might work in a crisis where extreme precision and urgency are needed, but it is not sustainable for long-term leadership.

- Employees under an icepick manager feel singled out and targeted.

- While this approach might yield quick results, it damages morale and loyalty.

- It creates an environment where people comply out of fear rather than commitment.

The ice pick approach may be effective on an individual basis when absolutely necessary, but it is never the right tool for managing an entire team.

3. The Butter Knife – Gentle, Controlled Guidance

A butter knife does not stab or squeeze. Instead, it smoothly moves the watermelon seeds to the intended target. In leadership, this approach is about direction rather than force. A butter-knife leader:

- Gently steers people toward the right path.

- Uses influence instead of pressure.

- Creates an environment where people feel safe, engaged and motivated to follow.

This method is the most effective because it builds trust and allows employees to move in the desired direction willingly, rather than through resistance.

Understanding Pressure in Leadership

1. People Are Like Watermelon Seeds

The harder you press, the more they slip away. The more freedom you give them within a structured path, the more likely they are to stay. Leaders who understand this create environments where employees feel valued, trusted and motivated.

2. Sweeping vs. Squeezing

When you try to pinch a seed, it escapes. When you try to stab it, you destroy it. But when you *sweep* it carefully, you keep it. The same applies to leading people:

- If you micromanage, they flee.

- If you intimidate, they resist.

- If you guide, they follow.

3. The Power of Gentle Direction

A butter-knife leader understands that people respond best to influence, not force. By moving with steady, controlled guidance rather than pressure, leaders can shape behaviors, build loyalty and create lasting impact.

Take People Where They Need to Go

Leadership is not about applying force, it's about direction. The best leaders don't force people into compliance; they create an environment where people *want* to follow. If you find yourself squeezing too hard or resorting to sharp, demanding tactics, take a step back. The butter knife approach is the key to guiding people effectively, without pushing them away.

Chapter 33
Don't Confuse Success with Legacy

Have you heard the statement, "If you want to make friends, go to the gym?"

The Gym: A Place for Personal Growth and Optional Socializing

The gym is one of the few places in life where you have complete control over your experience. You can walk in, put on your headphones, and focus entirely on yourself. You can lift weights, run on the treadmill or take a class, all without needing to engage with anyone if you choose not to. At the same time, the gym provides an opportunity to make friends if that's what you want.

Some people strike up conversations between sets, find workout partners or connect over shared fitness goals. Others prefer to stay in their own space, doing their routine without distraction.

Both approaches are acceptable because the gym exists for the individual, it's a place where you dictate your level of interaction. You are there for your own progress, and if friendships happen along the way, that's just a bonus.

Business is Different: It's About Service, Not Friendship

Unlike the gym, a business environment isn't designed for personal fulfillment or individual goals. The office is not about *you*, it's about serving others. Success in business isn't measured by how many friends you make; it's measured by how much value you bring to the table.

Friendship is optional at the gym. But in business, helping others is not optional, it's the foundation of success. Your role is to provide guidance, support, advice, and solutions. Whether you're leading a team, working with clients or building relationships with colleagues, your focus should always be on how you can contribute.

Finding the People Who Need You

Instead of seeking friendships, seek out those who need what you have to offer:

- Employees need leadership and mentorship.

- Colleagues need collaboration and teamwork.

- Clients need solutions and expertise.

- Organizations need people who drive results.

If friendships develop along the way, that's an unintended consequence, but it should never be the goal. The workplace is about contribution, not companionship.

The Pitfall of Seeking Friendships in Business

Some professionals make the mistake of treating work relationships the same way they treat friendships. They prioritize personal connections over professional impact. While workplace friendships can enhance teamwork, they should never interfere with accountability, decision-making, or business goals. If your primary focus at work is making friends, you risk:

- Losing sight of your responsibilities.

- Avoiding necessary conflict or feedback.

- Compromising business decisions for personal comfort.

Know the Difference

If your goal is to make friends, go to the gym. If your goal is to build a successful career, focus on service, leadership and making a meaningful impact.

The gym is about *you.* Business is about *others.* When you understand this distinction, you'll find success in both.

Chapter 34

The Police, The Judge and The Jail: The Essential Elements of Rule Following

Understanding the Dynamics of Rules and Rule Breakers

Rules exist to create order, structure, and predictability, but not everyone interacts with them the same way. Some people are rule followers, they obey policies without question, ensuring consistency and compliance. Others, however, see rules as obstacles to be navigated, challenged or even strategically broken. As a leader, it is crucial to recognize how people respond to rules and how to design systems that produce the behavior you actually want.

When faced with a rule, the questions to ask are:

1. **Who are the police?** – Who enforces the rule and how strictly?

2. **Who is the judge?** – Who interprets the rule and has final authority over its application?

3. **What does jail look like?** – What are the actual consequences of breaking the rule? Are they serious enough to deter violations?

The key is understanding that people don't just follow rules, they evaluate them. And in that evaluation, they determine whether compliance or noncompliance serves them better.

Two Types of People: Rule Followers vs. Rule Breakers

- **Rule Followers:** These individuals stick to the guidelines as written. They believe in structure, fairness and predictability. However, strict rule-following doesn't always produce the best outcomes. If you're a leader who only sets rules without clarifying the intent behind them, rule followers may comply in ways that technically follow the rule but don't achieve the desired result.

- **Rule Breakers:** These people are wired to question, challenge, and at times, circumvent rules. They don't necessarily break rules for rebellion's sake but rather because they see inefficiencies, inconsistencies or opportunities for better solutions. If they understand a rule well enough, they will also understand how to work around it, often without breaking it outright.

As a leader, you must be clear on the type of behavior you are trying to encourage. If your goal is strict compliance, you must design a system where the rule is effective and well-enforced. If you want adaptability and creativity, you may need to leave room for interpretation.

Understanding Consequences: The Police, Judge, and Jail Framework

When people consider breaking a rule, they don't just act on impulse. They evaluate risk, consequences and potential rewards. This can be broken down into three elements:

1. Working Out a Deal with the Police

Some rule breakers don't actually fear enforcement because they believe they can negotiate with or work around the enforcers. If enforcement is inconsistent or weak, the rule quickly loses its power. In leadership, this means if you set rules but don't enforce them consistently, employees will push boundaries, knowing there's a good chance of getting away with it.

2. Working with the Judge

Even if caught, some rule breakers bank on being able to appeal their case to a higher authority. If the judge (or leadership) is lenient, they may feel emboldened to push limits again. Leaders must be aware that if exceptions are granted too frequently, the rule's credibility erodes.

3. Evaluating What Jail Looks Like

The final piece is the actual consequence. If breaking the rule carries a light or insignificant penalty, people will weigh the risk versus the reward and may decide the risk worth breaking the rule. For example, if you have a $200 Bruce Springsteen ticket and you need to park illegally, but the fine is only $20, you might happily take the ticket.

People are always weighing:

- What will happen if I get caught?
- Is the consequence worth the benefit?
- How strict is enforcement?

If the cost of breaking a rule is lower than the perceived benefit, expect noncompliance.

Leadership Takeaway: Clarity and Intent Matter

Leaders must understand that rules alone do not create order, clarity and intent do. When setting rules in a business or organization:

1. **Define the desired outcome clearly.** Make sure the rule creates the behavior you actually want, not just compliance for compliance's sake.

2. **Establish fair but firm enforcement.** If you set rules but don't enforce them consistently, people will test boundaries.

3. **Understand human nature.** People evaluate rules based on risk vs. reward. If the "jail" is weak, expect more rule-breaking.

4. **Encourage smart decision-making.** Not all rule-breaking is bad. Some of the best innovations happen when people challenge inefficient rules and create better solutions.

Rules Should Serve the Mission, Not Just Control Behavior

The best leaders recognize that rules are only as strong as their enforcement and alignment with real-world needs. If a rule isn't producing the right behavior, it may need to be revised or eliminated. Understanding how people interact with rules, whether they follow them blindly, work around them, or break them entirely, allows leaders to create environments where the right behaviors emerge naturally.

Chapter 35

Reminiscing About How Great the Old Lightbulb Was While Sitting in The Dark

Throughout history, each wave of revolutionary change has been met with two reactions: fear and resistance by some, and curiosity and opportunity by others. These changes, whether industrial, technological, or philosophical, have the power to transform the world, but they also expose the biases we hold about what is possible, what is acceptable and what is worth pursuing.

The Legacy of Revolutionary Change

Think back to the Industrial Revolution. Entire industries and workforces were disrupted. Machines replaced manual labor, factories reshaped towns, and a new kind of worker emerged. At the time, many feared this change, believing it would ruin livelihoods and devalue human contribution.

Fast forward to the invention of the computer, then the internet and later the rise of FinTech and InsurTech. Each of these innovations sparked discomfort, doubt and pushback from those who feared they would become obsolete. And now, we face a new shift: the rise of artificial intelligence.

In every one of these transitions, those who allowed their biases to dictate their reactions often missed out on the immense opportunities the changes created. In contrast, those who embraced the change, partnered with it, and worked to understand its potential became the ones who shaped the future.

The InsurTech Experience: One Attribute, One Bias

I remember vividly when InsurTech began gaining traction. I was working in the insurance industry and had countless conversations with professionals about what it all meant. I'd ask them their thoughts, and time after time, I received the same answer:

"It won't last. Nobody wants to buy insurance online. Nobody wants to do all the work themselves."

What struck me wasn't the skepticism, it was the narrowness of it. They had latched onto one attribute of InsurTech and dismissed the entire movement because it threatened the way they worked. They saw it as a replacement, not a partner. They failed to recognize that InsurTech wasn't about forcing clients to work harder, it was about creating better experiences, faster processes and more empowered professionals. Fast forward 15 years and now we are seeing significant productivity improvements, sales enablement and improved client experience. These changes have increased the number of jobs, made some innovators millions of dollars and improved the lives of people in the insurance industry. Quite a different outcome than those who were biased against Insurtech in the beginning. That knee-jerk bias, the fear of change wrapped in the guise of professional wisdom, kept many from participating in the early stages of something truly transformative. The same is happening now with Artificial Intelligence.

My Personal Experience with AI and Writing

This book is a labor of love, built over many years of experience, mostly from my friend David. These isms, principles of leadership and life, have been shared with clients, teams, and friends. We've watched them spark personal breakthroughs, reshape careers, and guide people toward more meaningful lives. The value of this content is not in the method of writing, but in the lives it touches.

When I set out to write this book, I ran into a wall. My writing skills weren't strong enough to express the depth and simplicity of these ideas. So, I sought help. I took classes on ChatGPT and learned how to use prompt writing as a tool to shape the content. I didn't hand over the work, I partnered with a piece of technology to help express ideas that already existed.

Yes, AI produced the structure, flow and polish, but only after I refined it with dozens of prompts, edits and clarifications. It's not unlike hiring an editor or ghostwriter to support a traditional author. The core ideas remain mine and David's. The stories are our experiences. The intention is still ours. The mission is still deeply personal. Also, human time and energy is by far the biggest contributor to this book. David and I have spent more than 200 hours in time on this work.

But not everyone sees it that way. I've had friends and family mock the process. *"You're not writing a book, ChatGPT is writing it."* Or, *"You're just fluffing up pages to pretend it's something special."*

I find that response disheartening, not because it hurts my feelings, but because it reveals how quickly people let their biases stymie the potential for something that could be very positive for someone else. They see a tool and assume it replaces rather than enhances. They cling to traditional methods because they fear what change means about their own relevance.

In no way do I believe the writing of this book falls anywhere near the writing genius of great writers. This isn't a competition to prove this writing method to be better or worse than human creative and artistic writing. I consider it a new genre of communication that shouldn't be compared to the brilliance of successful writers.

Letting Go of Bias to Move Forward

Bias is one of the most subtle but powerful forces that can sabotage success. It convinces us that new things are dangerous, that new methods are lesser, and that embracing innovation is a betrayal of tradition. But the truth is, every evolution in our history has made life better for those who chose to understand rather than reject.

AI, like any tool, is only as good as the person using it. In my case, it has helped me give voice to ideas that might otherwise have stayed locked in conversation or memory. Now, because of this partnership, thousands more people will be able to access and apply these isms in their own lives.

The irony is that while others fear AI will replace the human touch, I've found it to amplify mine. It has not erased our work, it has elevated it.

Expand Your Lens

If we want to lead well and live fully, we must confront our own biases. We must ask whether our fear is rooted in logic or resistance to change. Revolutionary innovations are not threats, they are invitations. Invitations to do things differently, to serve more effectively, and to share ideas more broadly.

Don't let your biases close doors that innovation is trying to open. Your success may be on the other side of the thing you're resisting the most.

Chapter 36
How Can Such a Little Word
Mean So Many Big Things

Working It, Getting It – What the Hell is "It"?

We say it all the time without really thinking about it: *"He's got it." "She's making it." "I'm working it." "I made it."* But what exactly is "it"?

"It" is more than a placeholder for success. It's more than a vague nod toward achievement. "It" is the confluence of all things valuable, skill, purpose, energy, awareness, timing, discipline and impact. It's what happens when your talents, actions and mindset align with a meaningful goal. It is momentum, magic and mastery wrapped into one.

What "It" Is Not

Let's get one thing clear: *"It" is not just work.*

People often think they should be compensated or rewarded just for putting in the effort. But work without direction, without intention, without the right results, without ownership of "it," is just movement without meaning. Anyone can put in hours. Anyone can stay busy. But true value doesn't come from activity, it comes from effectiveness.

You don't get paid just to work. You get rewarded for working "it." And that means knowing what "it" is for you.

So, What Is "It"?

"It" is the shortest path to results. "It" is the X-factor. "It" is the center of the target. The thing that moves the needle. And yet, "it" looks different for everyone:

- For an entrepreneur, **it** might be building a business that solves a real problem.

- For a leader, **it** could be inspiring a team to exceed what they thought was possible.

- For a parent, **it** might be raising resilient, grounded children.

- For a coach, **it** is bringing the best out of someone else.

Whatever your world looks like, "it" is the clear, compelling, and valuable outcome you're working toward.

"It" is clarity. "It" is intentionality. It is knowing what matters most and giving it your best.

Working "It" vs. Just Working

There's a difference between showing up and showing out.

People who work "it" don't just clock in and go through the motions. They're tuned in. They're aligned. They're chasing something that's rooted in meaning and driven by outcomes. They:

- **Own their goals.**

- **Stay focused on results.**

- **Move with purpose.**

- **Bring value to others.**

When you're working "it," people notice. You don't have to say you have "it", they'll say it about you.

Make "It" Meaningful

Too many people chase things that look like success but aren't tied to anything meaningful. Titles. Applause. Paychecks. None of these are bad, but they're not "it."

"It" is internal before it's external. It's tied to purpose before it's tied to profit. If you don't define what "it" means to you, the world will try to define it for you. And you'll always feel like you're chasing something that isn't truly yours.

Get Clear on Your "It"

Ask yourself:

- What outcome matters most to me?

- What kind of impact do I want to make?

- What does success look like, not for others, but for me?

- What do I want people to say I "have" when they say I've got "it"?

Once you've defined "it," work it relentlessly. Sharpen your skills, build your energy, stay disciplined, stay focused, and above all, keep your purpose front and center.

Because when you know what "it" is, and you work "it", you don't just make progress, **you make "it".**

Chapter 37
Earning A Living Is Easier If You Understand How To Earn A Handwritten Thank You Note

The Author Brian Tracy said, "Successful people are always looking for opportunities to help others. Unsuccessful people are always asking, 'What's in it for me?'" Success, when viewed through the lens of Brian's wisdom, becomes less about personal accomplishment and more about impact. It's about genuine connection, deep generosity and sincere contributions to the lives of others.

Emma worked tirelessly as a teacher, pouring heart and soul into every lesson. She wasn't just teaching math or history; she was guiding young souls, shaping futures. Despite the long hours and modest pay, Emma measured her wealth in a currency few people understood: handwritten thank you notes.

One afternoon, Emma returned home, tired after a long week. Sorting through her mail, her fingers paused on an envelope that clearly wasn't a bill or advertisement. She gently tore open the flap to reveal a card, simple, handwritten and sincere.

"Dear Ms. Emma,

I don't know if you remember me, but I was in your class five years ago. At the time, my parents were divorcing, and life at home was unbearable. School became my escape. Your kindness, patience and belief in me got me through the toughest year of my life. Today, I received acceptance to my dream university, and I felt compelled to write to you first. Your support changed my life and I can never thank you enough.

Forever grateful, Marcus"

Emma felt warmth bloom in her chest, tears blurring her vision as she read and re-read the words. The note wasn't merely gratitude, it was validation, reassurance and proof of meaningful impact. She carefully placed it into a special drawer, atop other cherished notes, each representing a life touched, a heart reached.

Psychologically, the handwritten thank you note holds unique power because of the deliberate effort involved. Unlike an email or a text, writing by hand demands a conscious decision to slow down and reflect deeply. The act of choosing stationery, finding the right words and physically crafting each letter is evidence of genuine appreciation and thoughtfulness. This effort signifies that the gratitude expressed isn't superficial or fleeting; rather, it is deeply felt and sincerely communicated.

In an age of instant texts, fleeting emojis and impersonal likes, Marcus's handwritten note carried weight. It wasn't just ink on paper; it was emotional currency, tangible proof of having made a difference.

When we speak of success, we often default to financial or professional metrics. But true success transcends these measures. It lies in the quiet accumulation of gratitude, respect and emotional connection, the notes that arrive unexpectedly, humbly affirming our impact on someone else's journey.

So, ask yourself: do you have a collection of handwritten thank you notes? If so, embrace them as your true currency of success. If not, perhaps it's time to invest differently, to inspire, to connect deeply, and to generously share your gifts. Because at the end of the day, the most valuable currency we trade is measured not in dollars but in the heartfelt, handwritten acknowledgments of the lives we've touched.

Chapter 38

When You Are Offshore Fishing, Don't Concern Yourself with the Cost Of the Bait.

A Fishing Trip Gone Wrong

Tom, an executive and avid angler, decided to organize a fishing expedition with colleagues to pursue large game fish far offshore. He invested substantially, chartered a high-end boat and hired a reputable captain. Every detail was meticulously planned, except one.

At the last minute, Tom decided to economize on bait, choosing the cheapest option available. He reasoned, "It's just bait. How much can it matter?"

The day arrived, the sun rose magnificently and expectations soared. Hours passed without a single bite. Frustration mounted as nearby boats, with similar gear and location but higher-quality bait, pulled in trophy after trophy. The savings on bait, barely enough to cover lunch, cost them the entire fishing trip's success.

Tom learned a valuable lesson: scrimping on the final, critical component undermined the entire investment.

Business and the Cost of Quality

In business, this same scenario unfolds repeatedly. Companies often allocate significant funds towards research, technology, marketing and salaries, only to cut corners on crucial final elements. These are typically the customer-facing details that directly impact results.

Elena was an entrepreneur who launched a cutting-edge tech startup. She poured resources into hiring talented engineers, developing groundbreaking software and executing an ambitious marketing campaign. The market was buzzing with anticipation.

However, at launch, Elena decided to economize by selecting an inferior customer support platform and inexperienced staff, thinking these were trivial expenses compared to the rest. Once customers began experiencing minor issues, poor support magnified frustrations. Social media filled with negative reviews, customers withdrew, and a promising venture teetered on the brink of failure.

Elena had invested heavily in every aspect except the final, critical link, the direct customer experience. The modest savings on support cost her business dearly.

Investing in the Final Details

Leaders and professionals must remember that success hinges on excellence throughout every phase, especially the final stages that directly engage customers or produce outcomes.

Wise leaders understand that the final, direct-to-consumer or client-facing component can never be the place to economize recklessly. If the goal is substantial, the investment must be equally thoughtful and comprehensive.

The Leadership Takeaway

Next time you're about to launch an initiative or project, ask yourself: Am I tempted to cut corners at the very end? Am I risking the entire investment to save pennies on crucial details?

Remember the lesson from offshore fishing, when you've committed substantial resources, never concern yourself with the cost of the bait. Make your final investment count, and your efforts will be richly rewarded.

Chapter 39
Don't Ask a Favor of Someone That Doesn't Already Owe You One

In the popular TV series *Yellowstone*, there's a powerful scene involving John Dutton and a female friend who finds herself arrested. Anxious and desperate, she asks John, "Are you going to ask the judge for a favor?" John's reply is sharp and insightful, reflecting deep wisdom about human relationships: "I don't ask a favor of someone that already doesn't owe me something."

This powerful line speaks volumes about leadership and the importance of genuinely investing in others. True leaders understand that relationships aren't transactional moments; rather, they're continual investments in trust, respect, and goodwill.

Deposits and Withdrawals

Think of relationships as bank accounts. Every time you invest time, effort, empathy or resources into someone, you make a deposit. Every time you ask for help, you're making a withdrawal. Leaders who consistently make deposits rarely find themselves overdrawn.

Sarah is a leader who always takes time to mentor, encourage and support her colleagues. She's generous with advice, always listens and genuinely celebrates their successes. When Sarah encounters a major challenge, a critical client needing special attention, her team voluntarily rallies around her without hesitation. Sarah doesn't need to explicitly ask for favors because her "bank" is already filled from her consistent deposits.

The Wisdom of John Dutton

John Dutton's wisdom in *Yellowstone* reveals a key principle: leverage and reciprocity in relationships are built through genuine investment over time. When John indicates he won't seek favors from someone who doesn't owe him, he's highlighting an essential truth: true leaders proactively create goodwill and leverage through ongoing contributions and support.

Leadership isn't about immediate transactions or quid pro quo; it's about long-term commitment. Leaders who regularly show up for others, provide support, encouragement and genuine care; build reservoirs of goodwill.

Making Consistent Deposits

Leaders who thrive never rely on spontaneous favors from strangers or casual acquaintances. Instead, they carefully and intentionally build networks of meaningful relationships, making continuous deposits of respect, care and generosity. These deposits often cost very little, perhaps just empathy, kindness, advice or listening, but their accumulated value becomes invaluable when needs arise.

Jake is a senior executive facing severe health issues that have impacted his availability at work. Having spent years investing in relationships, celebrating birthdays, attending family milestones, helping colleagues in distress, Jake found overwhelming support during his own difficult times. Team members willingly stepped up, not out of obligation but out of genuine care and loyalty. Jake never had to formally request favors; his investments had built genuine goodwill.

Leadership Takeaway

John Dutton's insight is an essentialism of leadership and life: Invest deeply, genuinely and consistently in relationships, and you will rarely, if ever, have to explicitly ask for favors.

Remember, don't ask just anyone for a favor. Make sure you've invested so deeply in people that when the time comes, they respond naturally and willingly, knowing they're merely reciprocating your many thoughtful deposits.

Chapter 40
Dog Parking Is a Necessity

Have you ever watched dogs meet each other at a park? It's a hilarious, somewhat awkward ballet involving lots of sniffing, barking, growling, and inevitably, some very public relieving of bladders. Dogs aren't being rude or trying to embarrass their humans (though it might feel like it); they're just figuring out who's who. They're assessing safety, sorting out social ranks, and deciding who looks like the most fun to chase and play with that day.

Believe it or not, humans aren't much different. Sure, we skip the sniffing (thankfully), but our version of "dog parking" happens every time we step into a new meeting or network event. We cautiously assess each other through small talk, indirect questions, and yes, those awkward, overly firm handshakes.

Consider your last professional mixer. You arrive, scanning the room nervously, evaluating who seems approachable, who might be competition, and who could be the ally you desperately need. You exchange polite pleasantries, smile stiffly, and carefully drop hints about your job title, fishing subtly for theirs; it might feel tedious or superficial but it's vital groundwork. You're figuring out who you can trust, who you might enjoy working with and who could potentially be a threat to your goals.

Then there's the conference room showdown, the first time teams from different departments meet. You watch carefully to see who speaks confidently, who hesitates, who makes eye contact and who nervously checks their phone. You're reading the room like a dog sniffing out territory: who's secure in their position, who feels threatened and who is open for collaboration?

Acknowledging and embracing this initial dance, this human version of "dog parking", is crucial. Leaders who understand this dynamic make room for it. They don't rush it or dismiss it; instead, they recognize its value in building authentic, effective relationships. Once the sniffing around is done, the tension eases, trust forms, and people can truly engage, collaborate and play at their highest levels.

After all, nobody ever truly skips the "dog parking" phase; they just pretend they're not sniffing around. Better to embrace the humor, accept the awkwardness and let the fun begin.

Chapter 41
The Time Clock and The Scoreboard

Life is a game, complete with a time clock and a scoreboard. Unlike sports, however, the rules aren't always clear, and the goals are rarely straightforward. Your scoreboard reflects your definition of success, while your time clock is the window you set to achieve it. Both are crucial in determining fulfillment and satisfaction in life.

If your scoreboard focuses on ego, adulation or endless accumulation, you've chosen a relentless and exhausting game. This is a dangerous game, as it can never truly be won. There will always be someone with more applause, more followers, or a larger bank account. If unchecked, this endless pursuit can drain your energy and consume your life.

What truly matters? This question evolves over time. As you age, your scoreboard may, and should, change. Early in life, success might look like financial independence or career accolades. Later, it might shift toward relationships, health, spiritual growth or leaving a legacy. The flexibility to adjust your scoreboard as your values mature ensures continuous fulfillment and vitality.

The timeframe matters too. Setting realistic time clocks prevents burnout and promotes consistent progress. Ambitious yet achievable timelines fuel motivation without overwhelming you. Recognizing the limits of your physical and emotional energy keeps your goals sustainable.

Think of life as a series of seasons. Each season can have its scoreboard, reflecting your current priorities. Maybe youth is focused on career growth, midlife on family and stability, and later years on legacy and contribution. It's acceptable, even advisable, to evolve your vision. Holding rigidly to outdated ambitions stifles growth and undermines satisfaction.

Always having a scoreboard is crucial, though, it drives your desire to thrive. The clarity of having defined goals enhances motivation, discipline, and ultimately, happiness. Just ensure the scoreboard you choose aligns with your core values, remains flexible with your evolving vision, and respects the reality of your time clock.

Life, after all, isn't about perpetual striving without pause. It's about purposeful achievement, meaningful relationships and enduring impact. Know your scoreboard, respect your time clock, and you'll find not just success, but deep, abiding satisfaction.

Chapter 42
Find What is Hard

Life is hard for most people. We are faced with challenges almost immediately upon becoming a living creature, and challenges continue to come at us as long as we live. Challenges will face us in various areas, including survival, relationships, finances, health, and nearly everything we pursue. These difficulties will come at us, but every time we get through them, we find more joy on the other side. When we overcome adversity, we establish a history of overcoming obstacles and thus it gives us new confidence in our next challenge.

Adversity Defines You

Your ability to take a difficult situation and use your intellect, intuition, and skills to overcome it is what defines you as a person. Without struggle, you don't develop resilience.

Without hardship, you don't build character. Those who never face significant challenges often falter when adversity inevitably arrives. Ironically, avoiding challenges increases the likelihood of failure when it matters most. Growth only happens through difficulty.

Find What is Hard

The greatest pain comes when we seek comfort. Comfort lulls us into complacency, preventing us from pushing past our core objectives of success. The temporary discomfort of facing challenges is nothing compared to the long-term pain of missed opportunities.

Consider the difference between the two types of pain:

- The pain of discipline vs. the pain of regret. Eating right and working out might be hard, but it is far less painful than dealing with the long-term consequences of being overweight and unhealthy.

- The pain of perseverance vs. the pain of quitting. Earning a master's degree while working full-time is difficult, but the pain of quitting is far worse when you realize the missed opportunities that a degree could have provided.

The key is to *choose* to face what is hard. If you avoid difficult situations, life will eventually impose hardships on you that are far worse than the ones you could have voluntarily faced.

Facing Difficulty Allows for Success

History is filled with examples of individuals who became legendary because of the challenges they faced.

- **Steve Jobs** had IBM and Microsoft working against him, trying to crush Apple before it could rise. Instead of backing down, he used their opposition as fuel to innovate, ultimately revolutionizing multiple industries.

- **Winston Churchill** led Britain through one of its darkest times during World War II. He famously said, *"Meet success like a gentleman and reach adversity like a man."* His leadership was defined by how he faced obstacles head-on.

Without adversity, there is no victory.

A Young Man Changes How He is Viewed

A church van carrying middle school and high school children was coming down a mountain after a long day of skiing. The sun had set, and a storm had rolled in, making the roads slick and treacherous. The driver, a pastor at the church, was nervous as he carefully navigated the winding roads. Suddenly, the van began sliding sideways. The moment became terrifyingly clear, the van was going over the edge. Below was a 200-foot drop.

A heavy metal wire, attached to posts about two feet off the ground, was the only thing between the van and disaster. The driver shouted, *"Hold on! We're going over the side!"*

As the van plunged nose-first over the edge, it bounced, shook violently, and then came to a halt. The back wheels had barely managed to stay on the road, and the van was now nearly vertical, its front end shoved into the snow that had been pushed down from the top.

Everyone inside was in shock, frozen, terrified, uncertain if the van would hold. But one 15-year-old boy had the mental clarity to act. This boy was invisible to his peers. Just another kid who wasn't popular, not seen as anything special and the girls were not interested in him. Without hesitation or concern for himself, he opened the door and carefully stepped out, holding onto the van to keep from sliding. The slope was so steep that he had to carve steps into the snow with his feet to create a path back to the road.

Cars had stopped, and bystanders threw ropes down to assist. The boy methodically helped each child out of the van, guiding them carefully up the snowy incline, where waiting hands pulled them to safety.

Finally, he turned to the driver, who was still gripping the steering wheel, paralyzed by fear. Speaking calmly, the boy reassured him, coaxing him out of the seat and supporting him as they climbed to safety.

The church group learned a few hours later what had held them in place was nothing more than packed snow wedged against the undercarriage. It had been unstable the entire time because the wire had snapped. The van could have dropped at any moment. The tow truck was able to pull it back to the road, but the tow truck driver said he had chill bumps when he saw the broken wire. These kids could have easily ended up at the bottom of the mountain.

This boy, once an outsider, unnoticed by his peers, had stepped up in the face of adversity. His decisive action saved lives. Before that moment, he had been considered a "nobody." But in that instant, he became a standout among his peers, forever remembered by his peers and their families for his courage and clarity under pressure.

When "Hard" or "Difficult" show themselves, facing each head-on will allow for great happiness and success on the other side.

The Joy of Success Outweighs the Pain of Hardship

In the moment, struggle feels unbearable. But when you look back, the reward of overcoming hardship always outweighs the temporary pain. Success is built on the foundation of perseverance, resilience, and the willingness to face discomfort. The pain of hard work is temporary, but the satisfaction of achieving something great lasts forever.

So, ask yourself: Are you avoiding challenges, or are you embracing them? Because only through adversity will you rise.